Fa

100 Irresisti

Snacks

Jeremy Stone

Elevate Publishing Limited

Table of contents

Why this book?

For years we were told that fats are bad for us and to be healthy we should eat more carbs. But as our knowledge of science and nutrition advanced, we now know fats aren't as bad as we once thought! This is where the Ketogenic Diet comes in. Scientific studies now show the dangers and risks associated with simple carb diets. At the same time there are many studies that show the health benefits of a high fat low carb diet, including:

- **Increased Energy and Focus**

- **Increased Weight Loss**

- **Lowered Blood Sugar Levels**

- **Decrease in Hunger**

- **Lowered Bad Cholesterol Levels**

- **Reduction in Acne and Skin Inflammation**

After reading several Ketogenic recipe books I became disappointed because there was so much information that I wanted to know but wasn't included in the books. I found myself researching the nutritional information for each recipe I have been interested in just to make sure I wasn't eating too many carbs.

I wanted to make a Ketogenic recipe book that was helpful not only to beginners thinking about starting the diet, but also to people who have been on it for years, but are looking for cool recipes that had all the macro- and micronutrients right there in front of their face. Also, because time is so important all recipes are sorted from the least amount of time to the longest amount of time to prepare and cook.

This book contains proven tips and Shortcuts on how you can enter Ketosis. You will read straightforward information on the diet, what to expect, and lots of delicious recipes to keep you going.

Work your body into Ketosis and you will find an amazing way to lose weight, gain energy, and stay fit. As with any diet, make sure to consult with a physician before you start.

Also make sure to follow me on Twitter for all the latest news, tips and more recipes @JeremyStoneEat

Bonus: Ketogenic Diet – How A Nutritious Low Carb Diet Will Burn Fat Fast

As a special thank you to my readers, I am giving away free copies of my book Ketogenic Diet – How A Nutritious Low Carb Carb Diet Will Burn Fat Fast! Get over 30 quick and easy to make Keto recipes designed specifically for busy people like you. You will get awesome recipes for breakfast, lunch dinner and snacks with full nutritional information.

To get instant access to this book and more awesome resources, check out the link below:

http://bit.ly/1TCFJJv

As an added bonus, subscribers will be given a chance to get exclusive sneak peaks of upcoming books and a chance to get free copies with no strings attached. Don't worry, we treat your e-mail with the respect it deserves. You won't get any spammy emails!!

Introduction

Who doesn't like to eat sweets? In a modern day society most people eat too many sugar-based products. Unfortunately every day there is more and more evidence that sugar and sweets are actually harming us.

Being successful on a ketogenic diet means cutting out all processed sugar from your diet. Fortunately this does not mean that you cannot still enjoy delicious desserts.

This book is designed to inspire you with a wide variety of mouth-watering low carb "fat" bombs that can help you get enough healthy fats into your diet. That's why fat bombs are an ideal snacks in a ketogenic diet.

That most fat bombs should be looked at as occasional treats, and you should look at your daily macros when choosing what to eat. Here are examples of how fat bombs can help you in your diet:

- Take a fat bomb in between meals to reduce Hunger cravings.
- Use them to help reach your daily fat intake.
- Use fat bombs in the morning when you're on the go and don't have time to make breakfast.

To help you in choosing the right ingredients, I have also included links to the products that I personally use in my kitchen. Enjoy!

Chapter 1: Dessert Bars

Coconut Cashew Bars

These bars are very easy to make You can carry them anywhere and enjoy them at any time! If you want crumbly bars, process the nuts into small chunks before mixing with the rest of the ingredients.

Serves: 8
Prep time: 5 minutes
Cook time: 15 minutes

Nutritional Facts
Serving Size: 40 g

Calories: 205
Total Fat: 19 g
Saturated Fat: 7.8 g   **Trans Fat:** 0.0g
Cholesterol: 15 mg
Sodium: 64 mg
Potassium: 174 mg
Total Carbohydrates: 10.1 g
Dietary Fibre: 4.3 g   **Sugars:** 1.6 g
Protein: 4.2 g
Vitamin A: 4%   **Vitamin C:** 1%,
Calcium: 4%   **Iron:** 13%

Ingredients:
- 1 cup almond flour
- 1/4 cup butter
- 1/2 cup sugar free maple
- 1 tsp. cinnamon
- 1 pinch Salt

- ☐ 1/2 cup cashews, chopped
- ☐ 1 cup shredded coconut

Directions:
1. In a bowl add all ingredients and mix well.
2. Spread in a large platter evenly and freeze for 3 hours.
3. Cut in the forms of bars and serve.

Coconut and Cinnamon Desert

These muffins are very soft and moist. That is why it's hard to have just one! The ginger, nutmeg, and allspice will keep your taste buds tingling.

Serves: 12
Prep time: 5 minutes
Cook time: 15 minutes

Nutritional Facts
Serving Size: 24 g

Calories: 103
Total Fat: 9.7 g
Saturated Fat: 4.9 g   **Trans Fat**: 0.0 g
Cholesterol: 31 mg
Sodium: 109 mg
Potassium: 96 mg
Total Carbohydrates: 3.0 g
Dietary Fibre: 1.6 g   **Sugars:** 0.5 g
Protein: 2.8 g
Vitamin A: 1%   **Vitamin C:** 0 %,
Calcium: 4%   **Iron:** 4%

Ingredients:
- [ ] 1 cup almond flour
- [ ] 2 tablespoons coconut flour
- [ ] 1/2 teaspoon baking powder
- [ ] 1/4 teaspoon cinnamon
- [ ] 1/2 teaspoon salt
- [ ] 1/2 cup erythritol
- [ ] 2 large eggs
- [ ] 4 tablespoon coconut oil

- ☐ 1/2 teaspoon vanilla extract
- ☐ 1/2 teaspoon almond extract
- ☐ 1 tablespoon shredded coconut, organic

Directions:
1. Preheat oven at 355 degrees.
2. In a bowl add all ingredients and mix well until even.
3. Transfer into baking dish and bake for 15 minutes.
4. Cut into bars
5. Serve and enjoy.

Chocolate Biscotti

These biscotti are gluten-free, paleo friendly, and dairy free. These desserts are lightly sweetened. The biscotti will come out soft after baking. You can enjoy them immediately. Or, you can leave them longer in the oven at very low temperature to let them dry.

Serves: 8
Prep. Time: 10 mins
Cook Time: 12 mins

Nutritional Facts
Serving Size: 44 g

Calories: 225
Total Fat: 20.4 g
Saturated Fat: 7.9 g   **Trans Fat:** 0.0 g
Cholesterol: 20 mg
Sodium: 245 mg
Potassium: 258 mg
Total Carbohydrates: 7.7 g
Dietary Fibre: 4.4 g   **Sugars:** 1.2 g
Protein: 7.8 g
Vitamin A: 1 %   **Vitamin C:** 0 %,
Calcium: 7 %   **Iron:** 10 %

Ingredients:
- [ ] 2 tablespoons chia seeds
- [ ] 2 cups whole almonds
- [ ] 1/4 teaspoon salt
- [ ] 1/4 cup shredded coconut, unsweetened
- [ ] 1/4 cup coconut oil
- [ ] 1/4 cup cocoa powder
- [ ] 1 teaspoon baking soda

- ☐ 1 egg
- ☐ 1 packet of Stevia, which is equivalent to 2-3 tablespoons of sugar

Directions:
1. Preheat the oven 350F or 175C.
2. In a blender or a food processor, process the almonds and the chia seeds until the mixture forms into fairly fine texture.
3. In a large mixing bowl, combine all of the ingredients together until well incorporated, making a dough mixture.
4. Place the dough on a piece of aluminum foil.
5. Shape the dough into 8 pieces biscotti-shaped slices or long thin fingers. Alternatively, you can form the dough into a loaf shape, refrigerate it for about 30 minutes, and then carefully slice.
6. Bake for 12 minutes at 350F.

Blonde Cinnamon Bars

Oh, the perils of cinnabon! But wait! This well-iced recipe is a version that you can enjoy without guilt. Each bar is low carb and high in healthy fats. The best part? These bars are virtually sugar-free and have a measly 2.3 net carbs!

Serves: 2
Prep. Time: 20 minutes, plus 5-10 minutes freezing
Cook Time: 0 minutes

Nutritional Facts
Serving Size: 82 g

Calories: 308
Total Fat: 32.4 g
Saturated Fat: 24.9 g   **Trans Fat:** 0.0 g
Cholesterol: 0 mg
Sodium: 9 mg
Potassium: 222 mg
Total Carbohydrates: 5.3 g
Dietary Fibre: 2 g   **Sugars:** 2 g
Protein: 3.1 g
Vitamin A: 0 %   **Vitamin C:** 3 %,
Calcium: 4 %   **Iron:** 7%

Ingredients:
For the coconut cream mix:
- [ ] 1/2 cup coconut cream, cut into squares
- [ ] 1/8 teaspoon cinnamon

For the first icing:
- [ ] 1 tablespoon coconut oil

☐   1 tablespoon almond butter

For the second icing:
☐   1 tablespoon coconut oil
☐   1/2 teaspoon cinnamon

Directions:
For the coconut cream mix:
1. Line a baking dish with wax paper. You can also use cupcake/muffin tins with liners, if you prefer.
2. In a bowl, mix the ingredients until well blended. Pat the mixture into the prepared dish or the lined tins.
3. Freeze for 5-10 minutes.

For the first icing:
1. Whisk the entire ingredients together in a bowl.
2. Spread the mixture over the coconut cream mixture.
3. Place the dish or tins in the freezer.
4. Freeze for about 5-10 minutes.

For the second icing:
1. With a whisk, mix the ingredients together in a bowl. Drizzle the mixture over the frozen layers.
2. Return to the freezer.
3. Freeze for 5 minutes more.

Maple Butter Bacon Cheese Bars

The maple syrup adds the right amount of sweetness to every bite. If you opt to use a low carb sweetener instead of sugar-free maple syrup, it will make this treat virtually carb-free.

Serves: 2
Prep. Time: 15 minutes, plus 15 minutes freezing
Cook Time: 15 minutes

Nutritional Facts
Serving Size: 27 g

Calories: 126
Total Fat: 11.5 g
Saturated Fat: 6.9 g   **Trans Fat:** 0.0 g
Cholesterol: 25 mg
Sodium: 212 mg
Potassium: 56 mg
Total Carbohydrates: 2.6 g
Dietary Fibre: 0 g   **Sugars:** 2.2 g
Protein: 3.4 g
Vitamin A: 5 %   **Vitamin C:** 0 %,
Calcium: 1 %   **Iron:** 1 %

Ingredients:

- ☐ 8 ounces neufchatel cheese, softened
- ☐ 8 slices bacon, cooked, crumbled
- ☐ 4 teaspoons bacon fat
- ☐ 4 tablespoons coconut oil
- ☐ 1/2 cup unsalted butter
- ☐ 1/4 cup sugar-free maple syrup or 6 packets stevia powder

Directions:

1. Set aside 1-2 pieces amount of crumbled bacon.
2. In a microwavable bowl, combine all of the ingredients together.
3. Put the bowl in the microwave. In 10-second intervals, melt the ingredients.
4. When melted, stir to combine, and then pour into a pan or dish.
5. Freeze for about 15 minutes or until the mixture is set.
6. When frozen, remove from the freezer, sprinkle with the reserved crumbled bacon, slice, and then serve.

Cheese-Chocolate Coconut Layered Bars

Although Neufchatel and cream cheese have almost exactly the same taste, Neufchatel has slightly more moisture than the latter and it does not contain any saturated fat. Ketogenic-wise, both cheeses have the same 0.1 grams of carbohydrates per 1 ounce. Taste-wise, cream cheese is slightly richer tasting than Neufchatel. These two make an excellent substitute for each other.

Serves: 12
Prep. Time: 15 minutes, plus 30 minutes freezing
Cook Time: 15 minutes

Nutritional Facts
Serving Size: 42 g

Calories: 231
Total Fat: 25.0 g
Saturated Fat: 21.1 g   **Trans Fat:** 0.0 g
Cholesterol: 7 mg
Sodium: 60 mg
Potassium: 81 mg
Total Carbohydrates: 3.2 g
Dietary Fibre: 1.7 g   **Sugars:** 1.1 g
Protein: 1.5 g
Vitamin A: 2 %   **Vitamin C:** 1 %,
Calcium: 1 %   **Iron:** 11 %

Ingredients:
For the coconut oil layer:
- [ ] 2 cups shredded coconut
- [ ] 1 cup coconut oil

- ☐ 4 teaspoons Splenda or 2 packets stevia powder
- ☐ 1/4 teaspoon cinnamon
- ☐ Pinch sea salt

For the cheese-chocolate layer:
- ☐ 4 ounces Neufchatel cheese or cream cheese
- ☐ 2 tablespoons cocoa powder

Directions:

1. Line a shallow pan with wax paper (or foil). Set aside.
2. Over medium heat, warm the coconut oil.
3. When the oil is warm, add the remaining coconut oil layer ingredients. Mix until well blended.
4. Pour the coconut oil mixture into the prepared pan. Press the mixture to form a solid layer.
5. Place the pan in the freezer. Freeze until the mixture is firm.
6. When the coconut oil is firm, remove from freezer.
7. Melt the cheese-chocolate layer ingredients.
8. When melted, pour the mixture over the coconut oil mixture layer.
9. Return the pan into the freezer. Freeze for about 10-15 minutes or until set.
10. When the layers are solid, cut into 12 equal-sized pieces. Enjoy. Store the leftovers in the fridge.

Walnut-ty Chocolate Peanut Butter Cinnamon Bars

The chocolate, walnuts, peanut butter, and cinnamon with the undertones of vanilla make this dessert bar absolutely heavenly. The kick of the sea salt definitely enhances the flavour of this yummy treas.

Serves: 12
Prep. Time: 15 minutes, plus 20 minutes freezing time
Cook Time: 45 seconds

Nutritional Facts
Serving Size: 21 g

Calories: 125
Total Fat: 11.7 g
Saturated Fat: 5.3 g   **Trans Fat:** 0.0 g
Cholesterol: 0 mg
Sodium: 69 mg
Potassium: 132 mg
Total Carbohydrates: 4.1 g
Dietary Fibre: 1.8 g   **Sugars:** 1.1 g
Protein: 3.7 g
Vitamin A: 0 %   **Vitamin C:** 0 %,
Calcium: 1 %   **Iron:** 8 %

Ingredients:
For the chocolate bottom layer:
- 4 tablespoons coconut oil
- 4 tablespoons cocoa powder
- 1 teaspoon vanilla extract
- 3 teaspoons stevia or Splenda

- ☐ 1/4 cup walnuts, chopped

For the peanut butter top layer:
- ☐ 1/2 cup peanut butter
- ☐ 1 tablespoon cinnamon
- ☐ Pinch sea salt

Directions:
1. Microwave the coconut oil for about 45 seconds or until melted.
2. Stir in the sweetener, cocoa, and vanilla, mixing well until the mixture is smooth.
3. Fold in the chopped walnuts.
4. Pour the mixture into a dish or pan. Spread evenly.
5. Mix the peanut butter top layer ingredients. Gently pour over the chocolate mixture layer.
6. Sprinkle with sea salt.
7. Freeze for about 20 minutes or until set.
8. Slice into 12 equal-sized pieces. Serve.

Blueberry Cheese Coconut Cream Bars

Do you want some crunch in your treats? Just add crushed nuts for a crunchy crust!. Adding crushed almonds will only increase the carbs to 2.5 grams with 0.9 grams fibre and adding walnuts will only increase the carbs to 2 grams with 0.6 grams fibre for each bar. Enjoy these topped with whipped heavy cream or fresh blueberries.

Serves: 20
Prep. Time: 15 minutes, plus 1 hour freezing
Cook Time: 10 minutes

Nutritional Facts
Serving Size: 36 g

Calories: 178
Total Fat: 19.5 g
Saturated Fat: 14.4 g   **Trans Fat:** 0.0 g
Cholesterol: 29 mg
Sodium: 88 mg
Potassium: 23 mg
Total Carbohydrates: 1.5 g
Dietary Fibre: 0.0 g   **Sugars:** 1.0 g
Protein: 0.8 g
Vitamin A: 7 %   **Vitamin C:** 2 %,
Calcium: 1 %   **Iron:** 1 %

Ingredients:
- ☐ 1 cup blueberries, crushed whole or pureed
- ☐ 8 ounces unsalted butter
- ☐ 4 ounces Neufchatel or cream cheese, softened

- ☐ 1/4 cup coconut cream
- ☐ 3/4 cup coconut oil
- ☐ Splenda or any low-carb sweetener, to taste

Directions:
For whole berries version:
1. Pour the crushed blueberries into the bottom of the pan or dish.
2. In a saucepan, melt the coconut oil and butter over low heat.
3. Remove from the heat. Allow to cool for 5 minutes.
4. Add the remaining of the ingredients into the melted coconut oil-butter mixture. With a hand blender or whisk, whip the ingredients together, adding sweetener little by little.
5. Pour the mixture over the blueberries in the pan.
6. Place the pan in the freezer. Freeze for about 1 hour or until set.
7. Slice into 20 equal-sized pieces. Top with a few whole blueberries. Serve.

For pureed version:
1. Place the pureed blueberries, Neufchatel cheese, and coconut cream in a blender or food processor. Puree until the mixture is smooth.
2. In a saucepan, melt the coconut oil and butter over low heat.
3. Remove from the heat. Allow to cool for 5 minutes.
4. Add the sweetener. Pour the melted coconut oil-butter into the blender or food processor. Puree again until smooth.
5. Pour the pureed mixture into molds, cupcake liners, or tins.
6. Freeze for about 1 hour or until the mixture is firm.

Optional:
If you are using cupcake liners, add 1 teaspoon of crushed almond or walnuts into the bottom before pouring the mixture.

Macadamia Nutty Blackberry Cheese Bars

Blackberries are one of the fruits with the lowest carbohydrates. The macadamia nuts also add fiber and tons of healthy fat to this fruity dessert.

Serves: 12
Prep. Time: 20 minutes, plus 30-60 minutes freezing
Cook Time: 7 minutes

Nutritional Facts
Serving Size: 62 g

Calories: 275
Total Fat: 29 g
Saturated Fat: 22 g   **Trans Fat:** 0.0 g
Cholesterol: 9 mg
Sodium: 44 mg
Potassium: 100mg
Total Carbohydrates: 4.3 g
Dietary Fibre: 2.3 g   **Sugars:** 2 g
Protein: 2.4 g
Vitamin A: 3 %   **Vitamin C:** 6 %,
Calcium: 2 %   **Iron:** 12 %

Ingredients:
- ☐ 4 ounces Neufchatel cheese or cream cheese, softened
- ☐ 2 ounces macadamia nuts, crushed
- ☐ 1 cup blackberries
- ☐ 3 tablespoons mascarpone cheese
- ☐ 1 cup coconut oil

- ☐ 1 cup coconut butter
- ☐ 1/2 teaspoon vanilla extract
- ☐ 1/2 teaspoon lemon juice
- ☐ Preferred sweetener, to taste

Directions:

1. Press the crushed macadamia nuts into the bottom of a mold or baking dish.
2. Bake at 325F for about 5-7 minutes, or until the nuts are golden brown. Remove from the oven. Allow to cool slightly.
3. Spread the Neufchatel cheese evenly over the macadamia crust.
4. In a bowl, mix the mascarpone cheese, blackberries, coconut butter, coconut oil, lemon juice, vanilla, and sweetener until well combined and smooth.
5. Pour the mascarpone cheese mixture over the Neufchatel cheese layer.
6. Freeze for about 30-60 minutes.
7. Remove from the mold. Is formed in dish, remove and slice into 12 equal-sized pieces. Place the bars in a container with seal and keep in the fridge.

Coconut Chocolate Layered Bars

This coconut chocolate heaven can be made into Almond Joy bars! Just evenly space 12 almonds into the layers! Don't worry. The almonds will only increase the carbs to 5.5 grams for each bar.

Serves: 12
Makes: 12 bars
Prep. Time: 15 minutes, plus 1 hour freezing time
Cook Time: 15 minutes

Nutritional Facts
Serving Size: 29 g

Calories: 145
Total Fat: 15.3 g
Saturated Fat: 12.5 g   **Trans Fat:** 0.0 g
Cholesterol: 0 mg
Sodium: 4 mg
Potassium: 106 mg
Total Carbohydrates: 5.2 g
Dietary Fibre: 2.9 g   **Sugars:** 0.9 g
Protein: 1.4 g
Vitamin A: 0 %   **Vitamin C:** 1 %,
Calcium: 1 %   **Iron:** 17 %

Ingredients:
For the coconut bottom layer:
- ☐ 2 cups shredded coconut, unsweetened
- ☐ 2 droppers liquid stevia
- ☐ 1/3 cup coconut oil, virgin, melted

For the chocolate top layer:

- ☐ 3 squares Baker's chocolate, unsweetened (1 Baker's unsweetened chocolate bar is 1 ounce)
- ☐ 2 droppers liquid stevia (about 1 teaspoon. stevia powder)
- ☐ 1 tablespoon coconut oil

Directions:
For the coconut bottom layer:
1. Into a food processor using the S-blade, place the entire ingredients.
2. Process until the mixture forms into dough that falls away from the sides. Scrape down the sides when needed.
3. When sufficiently processed, put the mixture into the bottom of a 9x5-inches silicone loaf pan. For a thinner layer, use an 8x8-inches silicone cake pan.
4. Place the pan in the freezer while preparing the chocolate top layer.

For the chocolate top layer:
1. Put the chocolate and the coconut oil in a microwavable bowl. At 50% power, microwave the mixture until the oil and chocolate has melted.
2. When melted, remove bowl from the microwave. Add the sweetener and mix the ingredients until smooth.
3. Pour the melted chocolate over the frozen coconut layer, spreading evenly. Return to the freezer and freeze for about 30 minutes or until the layers are frozen together.
4. When frozen, turn the pan inside out, releasing the frozen mixtures.
5. Cut into 12 equal-sized bars.

Storage:
Place in a Ziploc and keep in the freezer.

Note:
You can choose to use semisweet chocolate and omit the sweetener for the chocolate top layer. However, this will increase the carbs to 7.6 grams and sugar to 4.7 per serving.

Dark Chocolate Almond Allspice Bars

With the added allspice, these bars have a deeper almond flavour. The cream makes these treats firm but moist. And if you like bars with some crunch you can add some almonds as well.

Serves: 2
Prep. Time: 5 minutes, plus 2 hours freezing
Cook Time: 0 minutes

Nutritional Facts
Serving Size: 31 g

Calories: 189
Total Fat: 18.8 g
Saturated Fat: 8.5 g   **Trans Fat:** 0.0 g
Cholesterol: 10 mg
Sodium: 3 mg
Potassium: 152 mg
Total Carbohydrates: 3.7 g
Dietary Fibre: 0.9 g   **Sugars:** 2 g
Protein: 3.7 g
Vitamin A: 2 %   **Vitamin C:** 0 %,
Calcium: 5 %   **Iron:** 4 %

Ingredients:
- 2 tablespoons almond butter
- 1 tablespoon heavy cream
- 1 tablespoon coconut oil
- 1 teaspoon cocoa powder
- 1/4 teaspoon allspice
- 4 drops liquid stevia

Optional:
- ☐ Almonds, chopped

Directions:
1. Into a container, mold, or cup, put the 2 tablespoons almond butter.
2. Add the remaining ingredients.
3. Mix until well blended.
4. If desired, top the mixture with chopped almonds.
5. Transfer in the freezer and freeze for about 2 hours.
6. When frozen, remove from the container. Enjoy!

Coconut Chocolate Bars

Once your body has adapted to the ketogenic diet, successfully switching from glucose to fat, your blood glucose will stabilize and you won't feel hunger pangs as much anymore. But once in a while, your taste buds will still want to eat something this delicious. These amazing bars are probably one of the best low carb desserts that satisfies your sweet tooth.

Serves: 5
Makes: 5 bars
Prep. Time: 15 minutes plus 2 hours freezing
Cook Time: 5 minutes

Nutritional Facts

Serving Size: 47 g

Calories: 203
Total Fat: 20.3 g

Saturated Fat: 17.7 g   **Trans Fat:** 0.0 g
Cholesterol: 0 mg
Sodium: 6 mg
Potassium: 133 mg
Total Carbohydrates: 6.2 g
Dietary Fibre: 2.5 g   **Sugars:** 3.3 g
Protein: 2.1g
Vitamin A: 0 %   **Vitamin C:** 2 %,
Calcium: 2 %   **Iron:** 16 %

Ingredients:
For the bar:
- ☐ 1/3 cup coconut cream

- ☐ 1 teaspoon vanilla extract, divided into 1/2 teaspoons
- ☐ 1 packet stevia, divided into 1/2 packets
- ☐ 1 cup unsweetened, shredded coconut

For the chocolate coating:
- ☐ 4 tablespoons coconut oil
- ☐ 2 tablespoons cocoa powder, unsweetened
- ☐ the remaining vanilla extract and stevia

Optional: instead coconut oil for coating
- ☐ 2 ounces cocoa butter

Directions:
For the bar:
1. Line a small cookie sheet with parchment paper. Set aside.
2. With a spoon or a spatula, mix the coconut cream with the shredded coconut, 1/2 packet of the stevia, 1/2 of the vanilla extract. Blend well. Put the coconut cream mixture into the prepared cookie sheet.
3. Shape the mixture into 1-inch thick 6x4-inches flat rectangles. You may need to use a kitchen wrap to shape the mixture.
4. Place the cookie sheet into the freezer. Freeze for 2 hours or until the mixture is frozen solid.
5. Meanwhile, prepare the coating.

For the chocolate coating:
1. In a small saucepan over low heat, melt the coconut oil until liquefied. \

2. Add the coconut powder and the remaining vanilla extract and stevia.
3. Mix for about 2 minutes or until the ingredients are blended well.
4. Allow the mixture to cool to room temperature, but still liquid.
5. Dip the frozen bars in the cocoa butter mixture, turning all the sides to evenly coat.
6. Return the coated bars into the cookie sheet.
7. Put the cookie sheet in the refrigerator to harden.

Storage:

For harder consistency, keep the bars on the fridge. For softer consistency, keep at room temperature. Be sure to keep the bars below room temperature because cocoa melts at room temperature. Use coconut butter if you want the chocolate butter to remain solid at room temperature.

Notes:

The sweetness of your bars will depend on the kind of stevia you are using. Always start with a small amount and taste test until your preferred sweetness.

Coconutty Dark Chocolate Coated Bars

These delicious bars are double-coated with melt-in-your-mouth yummy, crunchy chocolate! Each bar is low carb, vegan and Paleo-friendly. The short-cut chocolate tempering technique used in this recipe is also a handy method that you can use for your other recipes that need melted chocolate.

Serves: 24
Makes: 24 bars
Prep. Time: 15 minutes plus 3 hours freezing
Cook Time: 15 minutes

Nutritional Facts
Serving Size: 20 g

Calories: 96
Total Fat: 7.7 g
Saturated Fat: 6.3 g   **Trans Fat:** 0.0 g
Cholesterol: 2 mg
Sodium: 9 mg
Potassium: 56 mg
Total Carbohydrates: 7.3 g
Dietary Fibre: 1.2 g   **Sugars:** 5.2 g
Protein: 0.9 g
Vitamin A: 0 %   **Vitamin C:** 2 %,
Calcium: 0 %   **Iron:** 4 %

Ingredients:
For the bars:
- ☐ 1/3 cup coconut oil, organic, extra-virgin
- ☐ 1/3 cup coconut milk

- ☐ 1/2 cup Swerve (Confectioner's style) or erythritol-based powdered sweetener
- ☐ 1 cup coconut, finely shredded

For the chocolate dipping:
- ☐ 8 ounces dark chocolate (at least 85% cacao)

Directions:
For the bars:
1. In a medium saucepan, combine the coconut milk, coconut oil, and sweetener.
2. Heat the mixture over very low heat, constantly mixing, until the oil has melted.
3. Add the shredded coconut. Mix until well combined.
4. Pour the coconut milk mixture into a 9x5-inches (23x13 cm) silicone loaf pan.
5. Press the mixture into a tight even shape in the bottom of the pan.
6. Transfer the pan into the freezer. Freeze the mixture for about 3 hours or until solid.
7. When frozen, remove the pan from the freezer, turn it upside down over a clean flat surface lined with parchment paper. Press gently on the pan bottom, popping the frozen mixture out. Cut into 24 bars.

For the chocolate dipping:
1. Chop the chocolate into equal-sized small pieces.
2. melt 3 ounces of the chocolate chips in a double broiler or in a water bath. Heat it very gently, making sure not to let it get too hot, until it is melted, stirring occasionally.

3. Remove the melted chocolate from the heat. Add in 1 ounce of the chocolate chips into the melted chocolate, mixing until the texture is smooth.
4. Dip the frozen bars in the melted chocolate and then place on a cooling rack or on a parchment paper. Allow the chocolate to set.
5. Melt another 3 ounces of chocolate. When melted, add the remaining 1 ounce chocolate chips, mix until smooth.
6. Dip the bars for the second time in the melted chocolate. Return to the cooling rack or parchment paper. Allow to set.

For variation: Coconut-ty Dark Chocolate Coated Orange Bars
Mix grated zest of 1 large orange into the bar mixture before forming and freezing into bars and before coating mix 2 teaspoons of orange flavor into the melted chocolate.

Tips:
If you have no silicone loaf pan, you can form the bars in a plastic foil lined small ceramic baking dish. However, you will need to carefully cut the frozen mixture into bars while still in the dish because the plastic foil or the mixture would not come off easily from the baking dish.

To easily dip the frozen bars in the melted chocolate, hold the bars using 2 forks and then dip it. The excess chocolate will just run through the fork tines.

If you have no time to double-coat the bars, melt 6 ounces of the chocolate chips and once it's melted, add the remaining 2 ounces, and then mix until smooth. Dip the bars once, and then drizzle the excess melted chocolate over the bars.

Coconut Pistachio Almond Bars

These bars will require a little more effort to make, but they are definitely worth it. They are full of crunch with a suprising Chai flavour.

Serves: 24
Prep. Time: 15 minutes, plus 4-5 hours freezing
Cook Time: 10 minutes

Nutritional Facts
Serving Size: 35 g

Calories: 227
Total Fat: 23.5 g
Saturated Fat: 14.2 g   **Trans Fat:** 0.0 g
Cholesterol: 16 mg
Sodium: 52 mg
Potassium: 114 mg
Total Carbohydrates: 3.2 g
Dietary Fibre: 1.1 g   **Sugars:** 0.5 g
Protein: 2.6 g
Vitamin A: 4 %   **Vitamin C:** 1 %,
Calcium: 3 %   **Iron:** 8 %

Ingredients:
- ☐ 1/2 cup cocoa butter, melted
- ☐ 1/4 cup pistachio nuts, chopped
- ☐ 1 cup coconut butter
- ☐ 1 cup almond butter
- ☐ 1 cup coconut oil, firm
- ☐ 1 teaspoon coconut milk, chilled
- ☐ 1 tablespoon vanilla extract
- ☐ 1/4 teaspoon almond extract

- [ ] 1/4 cup ghee
- [ ] 2 teaspoons Chia spice
- [ ] 1/4 teaspoon sea salt

Directions:

1. Grease a 9-inch baking pan and then line it with parchment paper. Set aside.
2. In a small saucepan over low heat, melt the cocoa butter, stirring often. Set aside.
3. Except for the pistachios and cocoa butter, put the rest of the ingredients into a large mixing bowl. With a hand mixer on low speed, mix the ingredients, increasing to high speed, until everything is well blended, airy, and light.
4. Pour the melted cocoa butter into the mixture. On low speed, continue mixing for about 1-2 minutes.
5. Transfer the mixture into the prepared baking pan. Spread it as evenly as possible.
6. Sprinkle the chopped pistachios over. Refrigerate for about 4-5 hours or until completely set. Freezing it overnight is best.
7. When frozen, cut into 24 equal-sized pieces.

Chapter 2: Ketogenic Candies

Raspberry and Peanut Butter Truffles

These great tasting truffles are very easy to make. After baking, you can sprinkle the truffles with coconut flakes or crushed nuts.

Serves: 10
Prep time: 5 minutes
Cook time: 15 minutes

Nutritional Facts
Serving Size: 50 g

Calories: 193
Total Fat: 16.8 g
Saturated Fat: 5.1 g   **Trans Fat:** 0.0 g
Cholesterol: 13 mg
Sodium: 123 mg
Potassium: 198 mg
Total Carbohydrates: 6.9 g
Dietary Fibre: 2.3 g   **Sugars:** 3.0 g
Protein: 6.9 g
Vitamin A: 3 %   **Vitamin C:** 5 %,
Calcium: 1 %   **Iron:** 14 %

Ingredients:
- ☐ 1 cup raspberries, chopped
- ☐ 1 cup peanut butter
- ☐ 1 cup freshly whipped cream

Directions:

1. Preheat oven at 355 degrees.
2. In a blender add raspberries, peanut butter, whipped cream and blend until smooth.
3. Transfer into cupcake molds and bake for 15 minutes.
4. Serve and enjoy.

Almond Joy Balls

These balls are a healthy version of an old favorite candy bar. They are perfectly portioned into bite-sized balls. Store them in the freezer or fridge.

Serves: 4
Prep. Time: 15 minutes, freeze for 15 minutes
Cook Time: 0 minutes

Nutritional Facts
Serving Size: 21 g

Calories: 128
Total Fat: 12.8 g
Saturated Fat: 7.6 g   **Trans Fat:** 0.0 g
Cholesterol: 0 mg
Sodium: 1 mg
Potassium: 141 mg
Total Carbohydrates: 3.7 g
Dietary Fibre: 1.5 g   **Sugars:** 0.0 g
Protein: 2.3 g
Vitamin A: 0 %   **Vitamin C:** 0 %,
Calcium: 2 %   **Iron:** 7 %

Ingredients:
- 2 tablespoons almond butter
- 2 tablespoons coconut oil, melted
- 2 tablespoons cocoa powder
- 1 tablespoon coconut flour
- Splenda, to taste (or equivalent low carb sweetener)

Directions:

1. Mix the coconut oil and the cocoa powder.
2. Add the almond butter.
3. Mix until smooth
4. Add the coconut flour and the sweetener.
5. Form into balls.
6. Place the mixture on wax paper.
7. Freeze for about 5 minutes.

Optional:
When the balls are firm, dip each ball into melted chocolate. Freeze for 5 minutes or until firm.

Black and White Peppermint Cups

These peppermint cups are great as desserts or as treats for birthday parties and other celebrations. Each cup is very high in iron.

Serves: 2
Prep. Time: 15 minutes, plus 30 minutes freezing time
Cook Time: 0 minutes

Nutritional Facts
Serving Size: 97 g

Calories: 442
Total Fat: 45.1 g
Saturated Fat: 39.5 g   **Trans Fat:** 0.0 g
Cholesterol: 0 mg
Sodium: 15 mg
Potassium: 308 mg
Total Carbohydrates: 12.3 g
Dietary Fibre: 7.1 g   **Sugars:** 4.7 g
Protein: 2.8 g
Vitamin A: 0 %   **Vitamin C:** 7 %,

Calcium: 0 %   **Iron:** 59 %

Ingredients:
For the peppermint layer:
- ☐ 3/4 cup coconut butter
- ☐ 1/3 cup coconut shreds
- ☐ 1 tablespoon coconut oil
- ☐ 1/2 teaspoon peppermint extract

For the cocoa layer:
- ☐ 2 tablespoons coconut oil
- ☐ 2 teaspoons cocoa powder

Directions:
For the peppermint layer:
1. Combine all of the ingredients.
2. Mix thoroughly and pour into mini muffin tins or cupcake liners or molds, filling up to 1/2 full.
3. Put in the refrigerator for about 15 minutes or until hard.

For the cocoa layer:
1. Mix the ingredients.
2. Pour the mixture over the hard peppermint layer, filling the cups or molds.
3. Return to the fridge and cool until firm.
4. For serving, set in the counter top, allowing to soften for a bit for about 5 minutes.

Vanilla Lemon Melt-Aways

Even if you are not countingcarbs and sugar, you need this treat in your life. These desserts melt in your mouth like fudge! Each melt-away are virtually carb and sugar-free.

Serves: 12
Prep. Time: 15 minutes, plus 30 minutes freezing time
Cook Time: 0 minutes

Nutritional Facts
Serving Size: 21 g

Calories: 105
Total Fat: 11.3 g
Saturated Fat: 9.8 g   **Trans Fat:** 0.0 g
Cholesterol: 0 mg
Sodium: 1 mg
Potassium: 31 mg
Total Carbohydrates: 1.5 g
Dietary Fibre: 0.7 g   **Sugars:** 0.6 g
Protein: 0.3 g
Vitamin A: 0 %   **Vitamin C:** 5 %,
Calcium: 4 %   **Iron:** 5 %

Ingredients:
- [ ] 1/2 cup coconut butter, softened
- [ ] 1/2 cup coconut oil, extra-virgin, softened
- [ ] Juice and zest of 1 lemon
- [ ] Seeds from 1/2 of a vanilla bean

Directions:

1. Into a spouted cup, whisk all of the ingredients together.

For discs:
1. Line a 12-mold mini cupcake pan with parchment paper liners.
2. Pour the coconut butter mixture into the liners, dividing evenly.
3. Refrigerate for about 30 minutes or until the mixture is firm.
4. If desired, garnish with fresh lemon zest.

For mini cubes:
1. Line a loaf pan with parchment paper.
2. Pour the coconut butter into the pan.
3. Refrigerate for about 30 minutes or until the mixture is firm.
4. Cut into 1/2-inch cubes. Plate them with toothpicks.
5. If desired, garnish with fresh lemon zest.

Coconut Peanut Butter Chocolate Cups

These trifecta fat cups are very versatile. You can try them with cashew, almond, or sunflower seed butter. Before chilling the final layer, you can also sprinkle with chopped nuts or shredded coconut.

Serves: 12
Prep. Time: 15 minutes, plus 30 minutes freezing time
Cook Time: 10 minutes

Nutritional Facts
Serving Size: 21 g

Calories: 153
Total Fat: 16.6 g
Saturated Fat: 12.5 g   **Trans Fat:** 0.0 g
Cholesterol: 0 mg
Sodium: 25 mg
Potassium: 80 mg
Total Carbohydrates: 2.1 g
Dietary Fibre: 0.9 g   **Sugars:** 0.5 g
Protein: 1.7 g
Vitamin A: 0 %   **Vitamin C:** 0 %,
Calcium: 0 %   **Iron:** 4 %

Ingredients:
- ☐ 3/4 cup coconut oil
- ☐ 1/4 cup cocoa powder
- ☐ 1/4 cup peanut butter
- ☐ 1 teaspoon coconut oil

□   3 Stevia packets, to taste (or other equivalent low carb sweetener)

Directions:
1. Heat the 3/4 coconut oil until melted. When melted, divide into 3 bowls.
2. In one bowl of oil, stir in the cocoa powder until completely dissolved.
3. Add about 6 drops of liquid stevia. Stir to mix.
4. In another bowl of oil, add the peanut butter. Blend until smooth. Sweeten with liquid Splenda.
5. In the last bowl, add the 1 teaspoon coconut oil. Sweeten with liquid Splenda.
6. Divide the chocolate mixture into 12 small cups. Refrigerate for about 10 minutes or until firm.
7. When chocolate mix is firm, divide the peanut butter mixture over the chocolate mixture. Return to the fridge until set.
8. When firm, divide the coconut oil mixture over the hard peanut butter layer.
9. Chill until firm and until ready to serve.

Chocolate Coconut Layered Cups

These delicious cups are gluten-free and almost sugar-free. This version gets the recipes together with minimum effort and mess.

Serves: 10
Makes: 20 mini cups
Serving Size: 2 mini cups
Prep. Time: 15 minutes, plus 30 minutes freezing
Cook Time: 15 minutes

Nutritional Facts
Serving Size: 32 g

Calories: 179
Total Fat: 19.4 g
Saturated Fat: 15.7 g   **Trans Fat:** 0.0 g
Cholesterol: 0 mg
Sodium: 4 mg
Potassium: 113 mg
Total Carbohydrates: 5.3 g
Dietary Fibre: 2.9 g   **Sugars:** 0.8 g
Protein: 1.5 g
Vitamin A: 0 %   **Vitamin C:** 1 %,
Calcium: 1 %   **Iron:** 18 %

Ingredients:
For the coconut candies:
- 1/2 cup coconut butter
- 1/2 cup coconut oil
- 1/2 cup shredded coconut, unsweetened
- 3 tablespoons Stevia powder or low-carb sweetener of choice

For the chocolate topping:
- [ ] 1 1/2 ounces cocoa butter
- [ ] 1 ounce unsweetened chocolate
- [ ] 1/4 cup Stevia powder or low-carb sweetener of choice
- [ ] 1/4 cup cocoa powder
- [ ] 1/4 teaspoon vanilla extract

Optional: for the topping
- [ ] 3 ounces dark chocolate, sugar-free, melted,

Directions:
For the candies:
1. Line a mini muffin pan with 20 mini parchment paper liners.
2. In a small saucepan over low heat, combine the coconut butter and the coconut oil. Stir until melted and the mixture is smooth.
3. Stir in the shredded coconut and the sweetener into the melted coconut butter mix. Mix until well combined.
4. Divide the mixture among the prepared mini muffin cups.
5. Freeze for about 30 minutes or until firm.

For the chocolate coating:
1. In a bowl set over a pan of simmering water (make sure the bowl bottom does not touch the water), combine the cocoa butter and the unsweetened chocolate. Stir together until melted.

2. Stir in the sweetener and then the cocoa powder. Mix until smooth.
3. Remove the bowl from heat. Stir in the vanilla extract.
4. Spoon the chocolate topping over the chilled coconut candies. Allow to set for about 15 minutes.

If using dark chocolate:

Melt the pre-packed chocolate and then spoon over the coconut candies.

Storage:

Store in an airtight container and refrigerate or simply keep the container on the counter top.

Vanilla Mocha Pops

These trifecta fat pops are virtually sugar-free. The flavours of cream, coffee, and chocolate all come together for a sweet delicious treat.

Serves: 4
Prep. Time: 15 minutes, plus 45 minutes freezing
Cook Time: 10 minutes

Nutritional Facts
Serving Size: 85 g

Calories: 502
Total Fat: 56.3 g
Saturated Fat: 41.9 g   **Trans Fat:** 0.0 g
Cholesterol: 82 mg
Sodium: 170 mg
Potassium: 122 mg
Total Carbohydrates: 11.8 g
Dietary Fibre: 5.7 g   **Sugars:** 0.0 g
Protein: 1.3 g
Vitamin A: 19 %   **Vitamin C:** 0 %,
Calcium: 2 %   **Iron:** 4 %

Ingredients:
For the vanilla layer:
- ☐ 4 tablespoons unsalted butter
- ☐ 2 tablespoons heavy cream
- ☐ 1/2 teaspoon vanilla extract

For the mocha layer:
- ☐ 4 tablespoons coconut oil
- ☐ 1 1/2 tablespoons cocoa powder

- ☐ 1/2 teaspoon coffee extract
- ☐ 3/4 teaspoon liquid stevia or equivalent low carb sweetener

Directions:
For the vanilla layer:
1. Soften the butter in a microwave until it turns to liquid.
2. Stir in the heavy cream.
3. Pour the mixture into muffin tins or liners, about 1/2 full.
4. Place in the refrigerator for about 15 minutes or until firm.

For the mocha layer:
1. Mix all of the ingredients.
2. Pour the mixture over the vanilla layer, filling each cup to the top.

Optional:
You can top the mocha mixture with a very thin layer of melted dark chocolate.
Push in Popsicle sticks in the center and freeze for about 20-30 minutes.

Tip: When using pop sticks
Cover the muffin tin with plastic wrap. Push the pop sticks through the plastic. The plastic will help support the sticks if the mixture is not frim enough to support them.

Chocolate Coconut Candies

Made from virgin coconut oil, these candies are packed with heart-friendly good fats. These candies are completely sugar-free so you can enjoy guilt free!.

Serves: 6
Makes: 18 candies
Prep. Time: 20 minutes, plus 1-2 hours freezing
Cook Time: 0 minutes

Nutritional Facts
Serving Size: 47 g

Calories: 357
Total Fat: 39.8 g
Saturated Fat: 32 g   **Trans Fat:** 0.0 g
Cholesterol: 0 mg
Sodium: 157 mg
Potassium: 96 mg
Total Carbohydrates: 3.5 g
Dietary Fibre: 1.6 g   **Sugars:** 0 g
Protein: 1.6 g
Vitamin A: 0 %   **Vitamin C:** 0 %,
Calcium: 2 %   **Iron:** 4 %

Ingredients:
- 1 cup virgin coconut oil, cold-pressed, softened (not melted)
- 1 teaspoon vanilla extract
- 1-2 tablespoons sugar equivalent or sweetener of choice (1 tablespoon. sugar = 1 1/2 packet stevia powder)
- 1/2 teaspoon Celtic sea salt

- ☐ 2-4 tablespoons cocoa powder, organic, unsweetened
- ☐ 2 tablespoons almond butter or other nut butter

Optional: for sprinkling or rolling
- ☐ Desiccated coconut, unsweetened

Directions:
1. In a bowl or a food processor, mix together all of the ingredients until the mixture is smooth.
2. Scoop tablespoons of the mixture. Drop each tablespoon of mixture into a parchment or waxed paper or into a container with desiccated coconut.
3. Refrigerate the candies until solid. Store leftover candies in container with cover and keep in the fridge.

Sugar-Free Ferrero Rocher Copycat

This healthy version of the popular Italian candy is virtually no carb, gluten-free, and dairy-free. These balls are close to the real deal except for the absence of the wafer exterior, but they are so good you will barely notice the difference.

Serves: 12
Serving Size: 1
Prep. Time: 10 minutes, plus 1-2 hours freezing time
Total Time: 10 minutes

Nutritional Facts
Serving Size: 27 g

Calories: 161
Total Fat: 15.8 g
Saturated Fat: 3.1 g   **Trans Fat:** 0.0 g
Cholesterol: 0 mg
Sodium: 21 mg
Potassium: 194 mg
Total Carbohydrates: 5.4 g
Dietary Fibre: 3.1 g   **Sugars:** 0.9 g
Protein: 3.9 g
Vitamin A: 0 %   **Vitamin C:** 2 %,
Calcium: 3 %   **Iron:** 12 %

Ingredients:
For the balls:
- ☐ 1/2 cup homemade Nutella, recipe follows in Other Ketogenic Desserts
- ☐ 12 hazelnuts

For the coating:
- ☐ 2 ounces chocolate bar, sugar-free
- ☐ 1/4 cup hazelnuts, chopped

Directions:
1. In a dry skillet, toast the hazelnuts until fragrant. When toasted, remove as much skin as possible. Allow to cool.
2. Refrigerate the homemade Nutella for about 30 minutes. Scoop 1 teaspoon of Nutella, flatten like a mini pancake, and place in a parchment lined baking sheet.
3. Top the flattened Nutella with 1 hazelnut. Top with another 1 teaspoon flattened Nutella. Mold into ball shape. Make 12 balls. Refrigerate.
4. Melt the chocolate bar. When melted, stir in the chopped nuts. Mix well.
5. Line a baking sheet with parchment paper. Place a wire rack on the baking sheet.
6. Take 1 Nutella ball. Hold the ball with fork, dip in the chocolate coating, and take out, removing excess. Place the coated balls in the prepared wire rack. Repeat with the remaining ingredients.
7. Refrigerate until the coating is hard.
8. Individually wrap each boil with foil, if desired. Store in an airtight container and keep refrigerated until ready to serve.

Coffee Drops

These coffee drops are very handy when you want to spice up your coffee drink. Each drop is virtually carb-free and they are completely sugar-free. These fat bombs will certainly give you the fats you need to start the day.

Serves: 9
Prep. Time: 25 minutes, plus 1-2 hours freezing
Cook time: 5 minutes

Nutritional Facts
Serving Size: 37 g

Calories: 300
Total Fat: 34.5 g
Saturated Fat: 27.4 g   **Trans Fat:** 0.0 g
Cholesterol: 27 mg
Sodium: 123 mg
Potassium: 4 mg
Total Carbohydrates: 0.1 g
Dietary Fibre: 0 g   **Sugars:** 0 g
Protein: 0.1 g
Vitamin A: 6 %   **Vitamin C:** 0 %,
Calcium: 0 %   **Iron:** 0 %

Ingredients:
- ☐ 1 cup coconut oil, melted
- ☐ Ghee from 1/2 cup butter
- ☐ 1/2 teaspoon cinnamon
- ☐ 1/4 teaspoon sea salt

Directions:

1. Whisk all of the ingredients together until well combined.
2. Pour the mixture into an ice cube tray.
3. Freeze until solid.
4. Pop the drops into a glass container with cover. Store in the fridge until ready to use.
5. Take the 1/2 cup of butter and follow my instructions on how to make ghee

To make coffee:

Place 1 coffee drop and 10 ounces of a hot coffee into a blender. Blend well until the mixture is well combined and foamy.

Cinnamon Coconut Balls

These balls are decadent desserts. Coconut is easy to digest and is burned by the body as energy, not stored as fat. Use honey instead of stevia to make these balls Paleo friendly. However, if you are counting sugar, use stevia instead.

Serves: 10-12 balls
Prep. Time: 90 minutes
Cook Time: 5 minutes

Nutritional Facts
Serving Size: 49 g

Calories: 142
Total Fat: 13.8 g
Saturated Fat: 12.2 g   **Trans Fat:** 0.0 g
Cholesterol: 0 mg
Sodium: 8 mg
Potassium: 150 mg
Total Carbohydrates: 5.3 g
Dietary Fibre: 2.8 g   **Sugars:** 2.4 g
Protein: 1.4 g
Vitamin A: 0 %   **Vitamin C:** 4 %,
Calcium: 1 %   **Iron:** 21 %

Ingredients:
- 1 cup coconut butter (or almond butter)
- 1 cup coconut milk (canned, full fat)
- 1 cup coconut shreds
- 1 teaspoon stevia powder extract (or to taste)
- 1 teaspoon vanilla extract (gluten-free)
- 1/2 teaspoon cinnamon
- 1/2 teaspoon nutmeg

Directions:

1. Put a few inches of water into a saucepan. Place a glass bowl over, creating a double boiler.
2. Except for the shredded coconut, put all of the ingredients into the bowl. Heat over medium heat, mixing the ingredients until melted. Combine well.
3. Place the bowl in the fridge, cooling the mixture for about 30 minutes until it's hard enough to roll into balls.
4. Roll into 1-inch ball and then roll into coconut shreds.
5. Place the balls on a plate and then refrigerate for about 1 hour.
6. Keep refrigerated.

Spiced Chocolate-Coated Pecans

This tasty treat is paleo, keto, and diabetic-friendly. Each spiced chocolate-coated pecan halve is almost carb-free and completely sugar free.

Serves: 42 pecan halves
Prep. Time: 30 minutes, plus 1-2 hours freezing
Cook Time: 7 minutes

Nutritional Facts
Serving Size: 3 g

Calories: 19
Total Fat: 1.9 g
Saturated Fat: 0.6 g   **Trans Fat:** 0.0 g
Cholesterol: 0 mg
Sodium: 0 mg
Potassium: 18 mg
Total Carbohydrates: 0.7 g

Dietary Fibre: 0.0 g   **Sugars:** 0.0 g
Protein: 0.3g
Vitamin A: 0 %   **Vitamin C:** 0 %,
Calcium: 1 %   **Iron:** 2 %

Ingredients:
- ☐ 42 pecan halves (about 2.5 ounces)
- ☐ 2 ounces 100% dark chocolate, melted
- ☐ Spice you prefer (nutmeg, cinnamon, or vanilla salt)

Directions:
1. Preheat the oven to 350F.
2. Line a baking sheet with parchment paper. Arrange the pecan halves in a single layer in the prepared baking sheet.
3. Bake for about 7 minutes.
4. When pecan halves are cooked, remove from the oven, and allow to cool for 10-20 minutes.
5. With a fork, dip each pecan halves in the melted chocolate and then return into the parchment paper.
6. Sprinkle with a small amount of your preferred spice.
7. Place in the fridge for about 1-2 hours or until the chocolate coating is set.

Chapter 3: Frozen Keto Delights

Strawberry Ice Cream

This easy to make berry ice cream is paleo-friendly, dairy-free, gluten-free, and low carb. It comes out great right out of the blender. Each serving is packed with 48% of your daily vitamin C requirement.

Serves: 10
Makes: 5 cups
Serving Size: 1/2 cup
Prep. Time: 5 minutes, plus 1-2 hours freezing if desired
Cook Time: 0 minutes

Nutritional Facts
Serving Size: 125 g

Calories: 191
Total Fat: 18.4 g
Saturated Fat: 16.2 g   **Trans Fat:** 0.0 g
Cholesterol: 0 mg
Sodium: 12 mg
Potassium: 271 mg
Total Carbohydrates: 11.3 g
Dietary Fibre: 4.4 g   **Sugars:** 4.8 g
Protein: 2 g
Vitamin A: 0 %   **Vitamin C:** 48 %,
Calcium: 2 %   **Iron:** 8 %

Ingredients:
   ☐   2 cans (13.5 ounces) coconut milk

- ☐ 16 ounces strawberries, frozen
- ☐ 1/2-3/4 cup sugar equivalent (I used 18 packets Truvia)

Optional:
- ☐ 1/2 cup fresh strawberries, chopped

Directions:
1. Combine all of the ingredients together in a blender. Process until the mixture is smooth.
2. Place the mixture in the ice cream maker. Process according to the manufacturer's instructions.
3. If using fresh strawberries, add them before the ice cream is done to incorporate.
4. Serve immediately or put in the freezer for 1-2 hours to harden.

Chocolate Ice Cream

This is not your typical ice cream. This recipe is dairy-free and you only need 3 ingredients! Using coconut milk also makes this recipe very creamy. Also, this one is low carb with fibre and protein.

Serves: 4
Prep. Time: 5 minutes, plus 1 hour freezing
Cook Time: 0 minutes

Nutritional Facts
Serving Size: 105 g

Calories: 241
Total Fat: 24.7 g
Saturated Fat: 21.8 g   **Trans Fat:** 0.0 g
Cholesterol: 0 mg
Sodium: 55 mg
Potassium: 310mg
Total Carbohydrates: 7.4 g
Dietary Fibre: 3.3 g   **Sugars:** 3.5 g
Protein: 2.9 g
Vitamin A: 1 %   **Vitamin C:** 0 %,
Calcium: 7 %   **Iron:** 10 %
Vitamin A: 0 %   **Vitamin C:** 5 %,
Calcium: 2 %   **Iron:** 11 %

Ingredients:
- ☐ 2 tablespoons unsweetened cocoa powder
- ☐ 1 can coconut milk
- ☐ 1 teaspoon chocolate stevia
- ☐ Pinch salt

Optional:
- ☐ Cacao nibs

Directions:
1. Mix all of the ingredients in a blender.
2. Carefully pour the mixture into the ice cream machine.
3. Follow the manufacturer's instructions to make the ice cream.
4. Serve immediately.

Poppy Seed Lemon Ice Cream

If you are a fan of lemon poppy seed muffins, then you will definitely love this dairy-free, vegan cold treat. Poppy seeds are very high in manganese and calcium. They are also a good source of magnesium, zinc, phosphorus, and copper.

Serves: 8-10
Prep. Time: 20 minutes, plus 1 hour freezing
Cook Time: 0 minutes

Nutritional Facts
Serving Size: 94 g

Calories: 246
Total Fat: 23.5 g
Saturated Fat: 18.6 g   **Trans Fat:** 0.0 g
Cholesterol: 13 mg
Sodium: 24 mg
Potassium: 219 mg
Total Carbohydrates: 4.8 g
Dietary Fibre: 1.9 g   **Sugars:** 2.9 g
Protein: 7.1 g
Vitamin A: 3 %   **Vitamin C:** 10 %,
Calcium: 5 %   **Iron:** 8 %

Ingredients:
- [ ] 3 cups coconut milk
- [ ] 1/4 cup chia seeds
- [ ] 1/3 cup lemon juice
- [ ] 1/2 cup honey (or 1/4 cup xylitol or 1/4 teaspoon stevia powder)
- [ ] 1/4 cup ghee
- [ ] 3 tablespoons poppy seeds

Directions:
1. Put all of the ingredients into a high-speed blender. On high power, blend for about 1 minute or until all the seeds are pulverized. Chill and follow the instructions of your ice cream maker.

If you don't have an ice cream maker:
1. Freeze the mixture in a rectangular container. When frozen, dump the ice cream into a clean surface, and then cut into chunks. Put the chunks in a high-speed blender. Blend, tamping down the chunks to keep the chunks moving.
2. Pour the blended ice cream back into the container. Freeze again.
3. Alternatively, after pouring the mixture in a container, freeze it, whisking and then stirring every 30 minutes, until frozen.

Notes:
1. If you want your ice cream to be smooth textured, then add the poppy seeds at the beginning. Otherwise, add them at the very end for a crunchy whole poppy seed texture.

2. If you do not have a high-speed blender, grind the chia poppy seeds (for a smooth texture) first. Pour the coconut milk, ground chia and poppy seeds in the blender. Allow to sit for a couple of minutes while you assemble the other ingredients.

Coconut Cream Raspberry Swirl Popsicles

Who doesn't love popsicles? These Keto friendly treats are the ultimate snack on those warm summer days.

Serves: 12
Prep. Time: 20 minutes, plus 1 hour freezing
Cook Time: 0 minutes

Nutritional Facts

Serving Size: 73 g

Calories: 89
Total Fat: 8 g
Saturated Fat: 7 g   **Trans Fat:** 0.0 g
Cholesterol: 0 mg
Sodium: 6 mg
Potassium: 123 mg
Total Carbohydrates: 6.2 g
Dietary Fibre: 3 g   **Sugars:** 2.2 g
Protein: 1 g
Vitamin A: 0 %   **Vitamin C:** 12 %,
Calcium: 1 %   **Iron:** 4 %

Ingredients:

- 1 can (14 ounces) coconut milk, full-fat, refrigerated overnight
- 6 tablespoons low carb sweetener (9 packets Truvia)
- 1/2 teaspoon coconut extract
- 10 ounces frozen raspberries
- 3/4 cup water

Directions:
1. Turn the chilled can of coconut milk upside down. Open, pour off the coconut water into a container, reserving for another use.
2. Scoop out the coconut cream, transferring into a medium bowl. Add 2 tablespoons (3 packets) and the coconut extract. Beat until the mixture holds soft peaks. If the coconut cream is too thick to beat, add 1 tablespoon or more of the reserved coconut water to thin it a bit.
3. In a blender or food processor, combine the berries with the remaining sweetener and the water. Puree until smooth.
4. Add the berry mixture into the coconut cream mixture. Swirl the mixtures together, but do not combine thoroughly.
5. Divide half of the mixture into 12 small popsicle molds or into 8-10 large ones.
6. Tap the molds on the counter to release air bubble. Fill with the remaining 1/2 mixture. Tap again.
7. Push wooden popsicle sticks into each mold, about halfway. Freeze for about 3 hours or until the popsicles are firm.
8. To release, sit the molds in hot water for 10-20 seconds and pull the popsicles gently.

Mocha Ice Cream

This dairy-free ice cream is a delicious frozen delight. Plus, there is no need for an ice cream maker for this version. All you will need to do is blend and freeze. The xantham gum makes the texture of the ice cream soft and rich.

Serves: 6
Prep time: 120 minutes
Cook time: 0 minutes

Nutritional Facts
Serving Size: 50 g

Calories: 113
Total Fat: 11.6 g
Saturated Fat: 9.8 g   **Trans Fat**: 0.0 g
Cholesterol: 7 mg
Sodium: 16 mg
Potassium: 155 mg
Total Carbohydrates: 4.1 g
Dietary Fibre: 1.9 g   **Sugars:** 1.4 g
Protein: 1.4 g
Vitamin A: 1 %   **Vitamin C:** 2 %,
Calcium: 1 %   **Iron:** 5 %

Ingredients:

- [ ] 1 cup coconut milk
- [ ] 1/4 cup heavy cream
- [ ] 2 tablespoon erythritol
- [ ] 15 drops liquid stevia
- [ ] 2 tablespoon cocoa powder
- [ ] 1 tablespoon instant coffee
- [ ] 1/4 teaspoon xanthan gum

Directions:

1. In a blender add all ingredients and blend until smooth and creamy.
2. Pour this mixture into airtight box and cover with lid.
3. Freeze for 2-3 hours.
4. Serve and enjoy.

Lemon Gelato

This dairy-free treat is so delicious that you will want to enjoy a bowlful even in the middle of winter. This dessert is also packed with vitamin C, which boosts your immune system and helps keep the sniffles away.

Serves: 6
Prep. Time: 15 minutes, plus 1 hour cooling and 1 hour freezing
Cook Time: 30 minutes

Nutritional Facts
Serving Size: 155 g

Calories: 283
Total Fat: 28 g
Saturated Fat: 23.3 g   **Trans Fat:** 0.0 g
Cholesterol: 140 mg
Sodium: 27 mg
Potassium: 329 mg
Total Carbohydrates: 13.2 g
Dietary Fibre: 5.5 g   **Sugars:** 4.3 g
Protein: 4.5 g
Vitamin A: 3 %   **Vitamin C:** 32 %,
Calcium: 3 %   **Iron:** 11 %

Ingredients:
- [ ] 1 can coconut milk, full-fat
- [ ] 1 cup milk, non-dairy (almond)
- [ ] 4 egg yolks
- [ ] 1/2-3/4 cup granulated sweetener
- [ ] 3/4 cup lemon juice, fresh (2-3 lemons)
- [ ] 2 heaping tablespoons lemon peel, grated

Directions:
1. Whisk the egg yolks. Set aside.
2. In a heavy saucepan over medium-high heat, combine the coconut milk, almond milk, and sweetener. Bring to a simmer.
3. When the milk is simmering, reduce the heat to low.
4. Whisking the entire time, slowly whisk warm milk mixture into the bowl egg yolks.
5. Continually whisking the entire time, slowly pour the egg yolk mixture into the warm pan.
6. Add the grated lemon peel.
7. On low heat, continue cooking the mixture, stirring until it thickens and coats the back of the spoon.
8. Remove from the heat. Stir in the lemon juice.
9. Strain the mixture into a container to remove any lemon peel and seed.
10. Place the container in the freezer or fridge to cool.
11. When cooled, freeze in a loaf pan or run through an ice cream maker, or use the Ziploc method.

Ziploc method:
Pour the mixture in a Ziploc and then freeze. When ready to serve, put the frozen mixture into a blender and then blend until smooth.

Chocolate Chunk Avocado Ice Cream

Avocados are easy to find and packed with healthy fat. This ice cream is decadently sweet and rich. The bitter chocolate chips balance the sweetness and adds a crunchy texture.

Serves: 10
Prep time: 240 minutes
Cook time: 0 minutes

Nutritional Facts
Serving Size: 90 g

Calories: 236
Total Fat: 23.3 g
Saturated Fat: 12.7 g   **Trans Fat:** 0.0 g
Cholesterol: 8 mg
Sodium: 12 mg
Potassium: 439 mg
Total Carbohydrates: 12.8 g
Dietary Fibre: 7.6 g   **Sugars:** 1.3 g
Protein: 4.0 g
Vitamin A: 3 %   **Vitamin C:** 8 %,
Calcium: 3 %   **Iron:** 20 %

Ingredients:
- [ ] 2 ripe avocados, pulp
- [ ] 1 cup coconut milk
- [ ] 1/2 cup heavy cream
- [ ] 1/2 cup cocoa powder
- [ ] 2 teaspoon vanilla extract
- [ ] 1/2 cup erythritol, powdered

☐   25 drops liquid stevia
☐   1 cup chocolate chips

Directions:
1. In a bowl blender all ingredients (except chocolate chips) and blend until smooth.
2. Now add chocolate chips and mix well.
3. Transfer into airtight box and cover with lid, freeze for 4-5 hours.
4. Serve and enjoy.

Avocado Chocolate Pudding Pops

These treats are also a great way to make picky eaters eat avocado. They will look chocolate brown so the kids won't know they contain avocado and won't know they are eating healthy!

Serves: 10
Prep. Time: 15 minutes, plus 3 hours freezing
Cook Time: 0 minutes

Nutritional Facts
Serving Size: 75 g

Calories: 197
Total Fat: 19.8 g
Saturated Fat: 9.8 g   **Trans Fat:** 0.0 g
Cholesterol: 0mg
Sodium: 26 mg
Potassium: 366 mg
Total Carbohydrates: 9.4 g
Dietary Fibre: 6 g   **Sugars:** 0.7 g
Protein: 2.4 g
Vitamin A: 1 %   **Vitamin C:** 9 %,
Calcium: 2 %   **Iron:** 11 %

Ingredients:
- ☐ 6 tablespoons coconut milk, unsweetened (or almond milk)
- ☐ 2 tablespoons coconut oil
- ☐ 2 tablespoons cocoa powder
- ☐ 2 ripe avocados
- ☐ 2 ounces unsweetened chocolate, chopped
- ☐ 1/4 teaspoon stevia extract

- ☐ 1/4 cup low carb powdered sweetener
- ☐ 1/2 teaspoon vanilla extract
- ☐ Pinch salt

Directions:
1. Put the avocado in a blender or a food processor. Puree for about 3-4 minutes or until smooth. With a rubber spatula, scrape down when needed.
2. Add the coconut milk, cocoa powder, sweetener, stevia extract, vanilla, and salt. Continue processing on low power until well blended, scraping the sides when needed.
3. In a microwavable bowl, melt the coconut oil and the chocolate together in 30-second intervals on high, stirring, until the mixture is smooth.
4. Spoon 1/2 of the mixture into Popsicle molds and then tap the molds on a hard flat surface to release air bubbles.
5. Spoon the remaining mixture into the mold. Tap once again.
6. Press wooden popsicle sticks into the mold, about 2/3 deep.
7. Freeze for about 3 hours, or until set.
8. To release the popsicles, run hot water over the mold for about 30 seconds. Twist gently to release.

Chocolate-Coated Mocha Bars

These bars are a frozen version of mocha truffle bars. They are dairy-free and are a huge hit with kids. The gelatin will keep them soft during freezing.

Serves: 8-12
Prep. Time: 45 minutes, plus 3 hour and 40 minutes freezing
Cook Time: 15 minutes

Nutritional Facts
Serving Size: 108 g

Calories: 269
Total Fat: 26.9 g
Saturated Fat: 21.9 g   **Trans Fat:** 0.0 g
Cholesterol: 79 mg
Sodium: 22 mg
Potassium: 303 mg
Total Carbohydrates: 10.4 g
Dietary Fibre: 4.7 g   **Sugars:** 3.1 g
Protein: 5.5 g
Vitamin A: 2 %   **Vitamin C:** 4 %,
Calcium: 3 %   **Iron:** 16 %

Ingredients:
For the bar:
- 3 egg yolks
- 3 cups coconut milk, full fat, divided
- 2 teaspoons gelatin
- 1/2 teaspoon vanilla extract
- 1/2 cup low carb sweetener
- 1 teaspoon espresso powder, instant

For the coating:
- ☐ 2 ounces chocolate, sugar-free (or 80-90% cacao chocolate), chopped

Directions:
1. In a medium saucepan, add 1/2 cup of the coconut milk. Sprinkle with gelatin. Allow to stand for 2-3 minutes. Turn the heat to medium. Whisk until the gelatin is dissolved completely.
2. Pour in the remaining coconut cream. Add the coffee and the sweetener. Stir until the coffee and the sweetener is dissolved. Continue stirring until the mixture is 175F on an instant read thermometer.
3. In a medium bowl, whisk the egg yolks.
4. Whisking continuously, slowly add about 1 cup of the hot coconut milk mixture. This will temper the yolks.
5. Continuously whisking, slowly whisk the egg yolk into the saucepan.
6. Continue cooking until the temperature reaches 180F.
7. Remove from the heat. Pour into a bowl set over an ice bath.
8. Allow to cool for 10-15 minutes, until the mixture is no longer hot to touch.
9. Stir the vanilla in the mixture.
10. Divide into 12 small or 8 large Popsicle molds.
11. Freeze for about 40 minutes. Insert wooden popsicle sticks into the mixture, about 2/3 deep. Continue freezing for about 3 hours.
12. Melt the chocolate in a bowl set over barely simmering water.

13. Unmold the pops by dipping the molds in warm water for 10-20 seconds or running hot water over the molds for 20-30 seconds.
14. Put the popsicles into a wax paper lined baking sheet.
15. Place the baking sheet into the freezer.
16. One at a time, hold each pops over a bowl. drizzle with the melted chocolate, turning to coat all sides.
17. Return to the freezer.
18. Repeat the process with the remaining popsicles and melted chocolate.

Chapter 4: Puddings

Vanilla Crème Parfaits

These fruity, nutty parfaits are very easy to make and no cooking is needed to make them. This version is egg, dairy, gluten, grain, and soy-free. They are also vegan and Paleo-friendly.

Serves: 4
Prep. Time: 10 minute
Cook Time: 0 minutes

Nutritional Facts
Serving Size: 167 g

Calories: 399
Total Fat: 37.5 g
Saturated Fat: 22.1 g   **Trans Fat:** 0.0 g
Cholesterol: 0 mg
Sodium: 16 mg
Potassium: 439 mg
Total Carbohydrates: 13.6 g
Dietary Fibre: 5.5 g   **Sugars:** 6.8 g
Protein: 8 g
Vitamin A: 0 %   **Vitamin C:** 21 %,
Calcium: 4 %   **Iron:** 14 %

Ingredients:
- [ ] 1 can (398 ml) coconut milk, full-fat, chilled
- [ ] 10 drops liquid stevia (or 1 packet stevia powder)
- [ ] 1 teaspoon vanilla extract, pure, alcohol-free preferred

☐ 6 ounces berries, fresh
☐ 3 grams walnuts, chopped

Optional:
Ground cinnamon

Directions:
1. In the bowl of a stand mixer, add the coconut milk, vanilla extract, and stevia. Whip with the whisk attachment for about 30 seconds until well mixed. Set aside.
2. In a large bowl, mix the walnuts and the berries. Set aside.
3. Put about 3 spoonful of vanilla-coconut crème pudding into 4 jars. Divide 1/2 of the walnut mix between the 4 jars. Spoon a seconds layer of the vanilla crème pudding over the walnut mixture. Add the remaining walnut mix.
4. Sprinkle each jar with ground cinnamon, if desired.

Quick Avocado Vanilla Pudding

This is probably the easiest pudding recipe to make. All you need to do is blend the ingredients together. The avocado packs this pudding with heart-healthy good fats. This dessert is also a good source of fibre. The lime juice also makes this pudding a good source of vitamin C.

Serves: 4
Prep. Time: 15 minutes
Cook Time: 0 minutes

Nutritional Facts

Serving Size: 211 g

Calories: 445
Total Fat: 43.8 g
Saturated Fat: 25.6 g   **Trans Fat:** 0.0 g
Cholesterol: 0 mg
Sodium: 22 mg
Potassium: 761 mg
Total Carbohydrates: 18.8 g
Dietary Fibre: 11 g   **Sugars:** 4.2 g
Protein: 4.2 g
Vitamin A: 3 %   **Vitamin C:** 23 %,
Calcium: 3 %   **Iron:** 13 %

Ingredients:

- ☐ 1 can (13.5 fl. ounce or 400 ml) coconut milk, organic
- ☐ 1 tablespoon lime juice, freshly squeezed
- ☐ 2 Hass avocados, ripe, peeled, pitted and cut into chunks
- ☐ 2 teaspoons vanilla extract

☐ 80 drops liquid stevia (8 packets stevia powder)

Directions:
1. Put all of the ingredients into the blender. Close the blender lid.
2. Blend until velvety smooth.

Blackberry Pudding

This flavourful treat is lusciously decadent. This rich dish is beautifully coloured, with the berries peaking on the crust. The bitter and sweet flavours of the blackberries add a delicious citrus zing to every bite.

Serves: 4
Prep time: 5 minutes
Cook time: 20 minutes

Nutritional Facts

Serving Size: 102 g

Calories: 242
Total Fat: 23.4 g
Saturated Fat: 15.6 g   **Trans Fat:** 0.0 g
Cholesterol: 156 mg
Sodium: 112 mg
Potassium: 160 mg
Total Carbohydrates: 8.3 g
Dietary Fibre: 4.1 g   **Sugars:** 2.3 g
Protein: 5.1 g
Vitamin A: 12 %   **Vitamin C:** 13 %,
Calcium: 5 %   **Iron:** 9 %

Ingredients:
- ☐ 1/4 cup coconut flour
- ☐ 1/4 teaspoon baking powder
- ☐ 3 eggs
- ☐ 2 tablespoon coconut oil
- ☐ 3 tablespoon butter
- ☐ 2 tablespoon heavy cream
- ☐ 1 cup blackberries
- ☐ 2 teaspoon erythritol

☐ ¼ cup maple syrup

Directions:
1. In a bow add eggs and blend until fluffy.
2. Add cream, butter, erythritol, maple syrup coconut oil, coconut flour and blend for 1-2 minutes.
3. Now add blackberries chips and mix well.
4. Transfer into baking dish and bake for 15-20 minutes.
5. Serve and enjoy.

Coconut Pudding

Gelatin desserts are probably one of my favourite treats. Try to use gelatin made from grass-fed beef. This pudding is dairy-free. Top with whipped coconut cream, toasted coconut, or fresh fruit.

Serves: 4
Prep. Time: 15 minutes
Cook Time: 15 minutes

Nutritional Facts
Serving Size: 118g

Calories: 278
Total Fat: 27.2 g
Saturated Fat: 22.4 g   **Trans Fat:** 0.0 g
Cholesterol: 157 mg
Sodium: 25 mg
Potassium: 278 mg
Total Carbohydrates: 9.1 g
Dietary Fibre: 3.7 g   **Sugars:** 3.5 g
Protein: 5.8 g
Vitamin A: 4 %   **Vitamin C:** 5 %,
Calcium: 3 %   **Iron:** 11 %

Ingredients:
- ☐ 1 2/3 cup coconut milk
- ☐ 1 tablespoons gelatin
- ☐ 1/2 teaspoon vanilla extract
- ☐ 3 egg yolks
- ☐ 3 tablespoons honey (or 6 tablespoons or 6 packets stevia powder)

Directions:

1. In a small bowl, pour the gelatin and 1 tablespoon of the coconut milk. Set aside.
2. In a medium saucepan over medium-low heat, pour the remaining coconut milk and the sweetener.
3. Cook for about 3-5 minutes, stirring occasionally, until the mixture is hot.
4. In a medium bowl, whisking constantly, slowly pour about 1 ladle of the hot milk.
5. Continuously stirring, pour the egg yolk mixture back into the saucepan.
6. Cook for another 3-4 minutes, or until the mixture is slightly thicker.
7. Add the gelatin mixture into the pot. Whisk to blend well.
8. Pour the mixture into 4 ramekins.
9. Refrigerate for about 2 hours or until the mixture is set.

Chocolate Gelatin Pudding

Gelatin has many health benefits. It helps improve skin, hair and nails. It also has a detoxifying effect. It even helps reduce cellulite and wrinkles because it is packed with collagen, which helps keep the elasticity of the skin. This pudding recipe is also Paleo-friendly.

Serves: 2
Prep. Time: 10 minutes, plus 30-45 minutes freezing time
Cook Time: 5 minutes

Nutritional Facts
Serving Size: 108 g

Calories: 269
Total Fat: 26.9 g
Saturated Fat: 21.9 g   **Trans Fat:** 0.0 g
Cholesterol: 79 mg
Sodium: 22 mg
Potassium: 303 mg
Total Carbohydrates: 10.4 g
Dietary Fibre: 4.7 g   **Sugars:** 3.1 g
Protein: 5.5 g
Vitamin A: 2 %   **Vitamin C:** 4 %,
Calcium: 3 %   **Iron:** 16 %

Ingredients:
- [ ] 1 cup coconut milk (canned, full fat)
- [ ] 2 tablespoons cocoa powder
- [ ] 1/2 teaspoon stevia powder extract (or 2 tablespoons maple syrup or honey)
- [ ] 1 tablespoon gelatin
- [ ] 2 tablespoons water

Directions:

1. In a pan over medium heat, pour in the coconut milk, sweetener, and cocoa powder. Stir with a whisk.
2. In a small bowl, mix the water and the gelatin.
3. Pour the gelatin mixture into the pan. Stir until dissolved.
4. When the mixture is warm, pour into 2 small pudding cups or ramekins.
5. Place in the fridge for about 30-45 minutes to set. You can also place in freezer for faster setting.

Coconut Chocolate Chip Avocado Mint Pudding

The smooth minty pudding and the crunchy chocolate chips makes for a delicious contrast. This dessert is a good source of fibre, vitamin C, and iron. It is also packed with heart-healthy fats.

Serves: 3
Prep Time: 15 minutes, plus 1 hour freezing
Cook Time: 0 minutes

Nutritional Facts
Serving Size: 234 g

Calories: 748
Total Fat: 80.1 g
Saturated Fat: 61.3 g   **Trans Fat:** 0.0 g
Cholesterol: 0 mg
Sodium: 24 mg
Potassium: 709 mg
Total Carbohydrates: 14.7 g
Dietary Fibre: 8.3 g   **Sugars:** 4.6 g
Protein: 4.5 g
Vitamin A: 2 %   **Vitamin C:** 17 %,
Calcium: 3 %   **Iron:** 16 %

Ingredients:
For the chips:
- ☐ 1/2 cup coconut oil, melted
- ☐ 1 tablespoon cocoa powder
- ☐ 3 drops liquid stevia (or 1/4 packet stevia powder)

For the pudding:
- ☐ 1 can (13.5 ounces) coconut milk, full-fat
- ☐ 1 teaspoon peppermint oil
- ☐ 1 large avocado, pitted
- ☐ 10 drops liquid stevia (or 1 packet stevia powder)

Directions:
For the chips:
1. Grease or line a small flat container with parchment paper.
2. Put all of the ingredients in a small mixing bowl. Fork until the mixture is smooth or blend with a whisk.
3. Pour into the prepared container.
4. Put in the fridge for about 1 hour or until the mixture is set.
5. When set, remove from the fridge.
6. With a sharp knife, chop the chips into rough pieces.

For the pudding:
1. Put all of the ingredients into the blender. Process until the mixture is smooth.
2. Fold the chips into the pudding. Place the pudding mixture into the fridge.
3. Chill for about 1 hour.

Chapter 5: Cookies

Browned Chocolate Chip Buttered Cookie

Try this delicious one skillet recipe to make a mouth-watering treat that your taste buds will thank you for!

Serves: 12
Prep. Time: 30 minutes
Cook Time: 30 minutes

Nutrition Facts
Serving Size: 38 g

Calories: 198
Total Fat: 16.8 g
Saturated Fat: 6.1 g   **Trans Fat:** 0 g
Cholesterol: 36 mg
Sodium: 139 m g
Potassium: 182 mg
Total Carbohydrates: 9.5 g
Dietary Fiber: 3.2 g   **Sugar:** 4.8 g
Protein: 4.7 g
Vitamin A: 5%   **Vitamin C:** 0%
Calcium: 5%   **Iron:** 7%

Ingredients:
- ☐ 1 large egg
- ☐ 1 teaspoon pure vanilla extract
- ☐ 1/2 cup butter
- ☐ 1/2 cup chocolate chips, sugar free
- ☐ 1/2 teaspoon sea salt

- ☐ 1/4 cup Splenda or natural granulated sweetener
- ☐ 2 cups almond flour
- ☐ 2 tablespoons coconut sugar

Directions:
1. Preheat the oven to 350F or 176C.
2. In a 9-inch cast iron skillet, heat the butter until bubbling. Reduce the heat to low. Cover pan. Cook the butter, stirring occasionally, until it starts to brown. When brown, remove the skillet from the heat. Allow to cool for about 5 minutes.
3. Meanwhile, whisk the eggs and the vanilla extract together. Add in the coconut sugar and the sweetener. Whisk together until combined. When the butter is cool, add into the egg mixture. Combine well.
4. Sift in the almond flour, pressing any lumps gently over the sieve. Add in the salt and half of the chocolate chips. Mix gently until the batter is creamy. Spoon batter into the skillet. Top with the remaining chocolate chips.
5. Bake for about 25-30 minutes or until the top is set and a toothpick comes out clean when inserted into the center. Serve with frozen yogurt or no sugar ice cream.

Frost Bite Cookies

What's even better than cookies? Cookies with white chocolate coating, of course! These Paleo-friendly treats are virtually sugar-free and are a good source of fibre. Yum, yum, yum!

Serves: 24
Prep. Time: 5 mins
Cook Time: 11 mins

Nutritional Facts

Serving Size: 21 g

Calories: 83
Total Fat: 8.5 g
Saturated Fat: 5.2 g   **Trans Fat:** 0.0 g
Cholesterol: 34 mg
Sodium: 99 mg
Potassium: 63 mg
Total Carbohydrates: 6.9 g
Dietary Fibre: 3.6 g   **Sugars:** 0.9 g
Protein: 1.2 g
Vitamin A: 5 %   **Vitamin C:** 0 %,
Calcium: 1 %   **Iron:** 3 %

Ingredients:
For the cookies:
- ☐ 1 3/4 cup Swerve or your preferred low carb sweetener
- ☐ 1 cup unsweetened cocoa powder
- ☐ 1/2 cup butter or coconut oil
- ☐ 1/4 teaspoon sea salt
- ☐ 2 eggs

- ☐ 2 teaspoon vanilla (or other extract - Cherry extract is good for this)

For the frost bite dip:
- ☐ 4 ounces cocoa butter
- ☐ 1 teaspoon vanilla extract
- ☐ 1/4 teaspoon almond extract (or other extract - Cherry extract is good for this)
- ☐ 1/4 teaspoon sea salt
- ☐ 2/3 cup Swerve confectioners

Directions:
For the cookies:
1. Preheat the oven to 350F.
2. In a medium mixing bowl, mix the butter or oil and the sweetener together.
3. Add the eggs and stir until the mixture is well combined.
4. Add the remaining cookies ingredients. Mix well until well combined.
5. Form the cookie mixture into 2-inch balls.
6. Place the balls about 2 inches apart from each other in a cookie sheet. Flatten the balls.
7. Bake for 10 minutes. When cooked, allow to cool inside the cookie sheet before removing. Meanwhile, make the dip.

For the frost bite dip:
1. In a double boiler, put the cocoa butter. Heat on medium-high heat until melted. Alternatively, place in a microwavable bowl. Heat on high for 1 minute until melted. If some parts are still solid, heat again in 10-second increments.

2. When melted, stir in the sweetener, extracts, and salt.
3. Allow the mixture to cool a little bit, about spreading consistency. If the mixture is still too hot, it will separate when you spread it.
4. When cool to spreading consistency, spread the mixture over the bottom of each cookie using a knife. Make sure to cover the surface completely.
5. With the chocolate side up, return the cookies on the baking sheet.
6. Place the baking sheet in the freezer for about 2 minutes to set the white chocolate faster. You can let it cool in the countertop.

Chocolate Chunk Cookies

These desserts are scrumptious and they will remind you of Chips Ahoy. These low-carb versions of my all-time childhood favourite cookies. They are crisp on the outside, yet soft on the inside. Dunk in almond or coconut milk as a snack.

Serves: 8
Prep time: 5 minutes
Cook time: 15 minutes

Nutritional Facts
Serving Size: 60 g

Calories: 285
Total Fat: 27.8 g
Saturated Fat: 13.8 g   **Trans Fat**: 0.0g
Cholesterol: 77 mg
Sodium: 107 mg
Potassium: 282 mg
Total Carbohydrates: 8.8 g
Dietary Fibre: 4.7 g   **Sugars:** 1.0 g
Protein: 7.9 g
Vitamin A: 8 %   **Vitamin C:** 0 %,
Calcium: 7 %   **Iron:** 21 %

Ingredients:
- 1 cup almond flour
- 3 tablespoons unflavored whey protein
- 2 tablespoons coconut flour
- 8 tablespoon unsalted butter
- 2 teaspoon quality vanilla extract
- 1/4 cup erythritol
- 10 drops liquid stevia

- ☐ 1/2 teaspoon baking powder
- ☐ 2 large eggs
- ☐ 1 cup chocolate chunks

Directions:
1. In a blender add eggs and blend until fluffy.
2. Now add butter and blend again.
3. Add all remaining ingredients and mix well.
4. Make small round cookies and place into baking dish.
5. Bake for 15-20 minutes.
6. Serve and enjoy.

Chocolate Macaroon Cookies

These macaroons are super easy and super yummy! The combination of coconut and chocolate is wonderful. They are chocolatey sweet delectably chewy.

Serves: 10
Prep time: 5 minutes
Cook time: 15 minutes

Nutritional Facts
Serving Size: 38 g

Calories: 156
Total Fat: 14.6 g
Saturated Fat: 8.4 g   **Trans Fat**: 0.0g
Cholesterol: 37 mg
Sodium: 75 mg
Potassium: 171 mg
Total Carbohydrates: 5.4 g
Dietary Fibre: 3.0 g   **Sugars:** 1.2 g
Protein: 4.0 g
Vitamin A: 1 %   **Vitamin C:** 1 %,
Calcium: 3 %   **Iron:** 12 %

Ingredients:
- ☐ 1 cup almond flour
- ☐ 3 tablespoon coconut Flour
- ☐ 1/4 cup cocoa powder
- ☐ 1/3 cup erythritol
- ☐ 1 cup unsweetened shredded coconut
- ☐ 1/4 teaspoon salt
- ☐ 2 large eggs
- ☐ 1/4 cup coconut oil

☐   1 teaspoon vanilla extract

Directions:
1. Preheat oven at 355 degrees.
2. In a bow add all ingredients and mix thoroughly.
3. Make 10-12 small round balls and transfer into baking dish.
4. Bake for 15 minutes.
5. Serve and enjoy.

Coconut and Almond flour Cookies

Almond flour is the secret ingredient of these tender crisp cookies. If you prefer them crispier, allow them to cool for a few minutes before munching. Store them in an airtight container and keep at room temperature.

Serves: 8
Prep time: 5 minutes
Cook time: 15 minutes

Nutritional Facts
Serving Size: 66 g

Calories: 285
Total Fat: 26.2 g
Saturated Fat: 11.3 g   **Trans Fat:** 0.0g
Cholesterol: 59 mg
Sodium: 65 mg
Potassium: 268 mg
Total Carbohydrates: 8.7 g
Dietary Fibre: 4.8 g   **Sugars:** 2.6 g
Protein: 7.3 g
Vitamin A: 5 %   **Vitamin C:** 2 %,
Calcium: 8 %   **Iron:** 22 %

Ingredients:
- ☐ 1 cup almond flour
- ☐ 2 eggs
- ☐ 1 cup coconut powder
- ☐ ½ teaspoon vanilla extract
- ☐ ¼ cup butter
- ☐ ½ cup cream milk

Directions:
1. Preheat oven at 355 degrees.
2. In a bowl add eggs and beat until smooth.
3. Add butter almond powder, coconut powder, cream milk, vanilla extract and beat for 1 minute.
4. Transfer into baking dish and bake for 15 minutes.
5. Serve and enjoy.

Lemon Coconut Butter Cookies

Lemon and coconut butter make the perfect pair. The combination makes for a melt in your mouth cookie! Coconut butter is also an excellent alternative for nut butters and flour.

Serves: 12
Prep. Time: 10 minutes
Cook Time: 10 minutes

Nutritional Facts
Serving Size: 28 g

Calories: 76
Total Fat: 6.7 g
Saturated Fat: 3.4 g   **Trans Fat:** 0.0 g
Cholesterol: 14 mg
Sodium: 28 mg
Potassium: 130 mg
Total Carbohydrates: 5.5 g
Dietary Fibre: 2.5 g   **Sugars:** 0.8 g
Protein: 2.0 g
Vitamin A: 0 %   **Vitamin C:** 6 %,
Calcium: 4 %   **Iron:** 9 %

Ingredients:
- 3/4 cup coconut butter, softened
- 2/3 – 3/4cup Swerve
- 1/4 cup cashew butter (I prefer fresh grind, jarred has added oils)
- 1 teaspoon baking powder (gluten and corn free)
- 1 tablespoon grated lemon peel
- 1 egg

- ☐ 1/4 cup FRESH lemon juice, strained (about 1 lemon)
- ☐ Dash of sea salt

Directions:
1. Place the softened coconut butter into a blender and food processor. Pulse until the mixture smooth.
2. Add in the remaining ingredients. Process until well combined without a trace of lemon peel in the mixture.
3. If your mixture is too soft to mold, refrigerate it for a few minutes to harden.
4. Roll the mixture into 1-inch balls. Place the balls in a parchment lined cookie sheet. Lightly press on the balls to flatten them.
5. Bake at 350F for about 10-12 minutes or until the edges of the cookies are slightly brown.
6. Allow the cookies to cool in the cookie sheet for a few minutes and then transfer on a cooling rack.
7. Store the cookies in an airtight container. If you want harder cookies, then keep in the refrigerator.

Note:
To make your own coconut butter, blend shredded coconut for about 20 minutes or until you make a paste. You can season the butter with salt, if desired.

Spiced Ginger Cookies

These cookies are dairy-free, gluten-free, and paleo-friendly. They are virtually sugar-free and are packed with the many health benefits of cinnamon, ginger, and chia seeds.

Serves: 12 medium-sized cookies
Prep. Time: 10 mins
Cook Time: 15 mins

Nutritional Facts
Serving Size: 29 g

Calories: 148
Total Fat: 12.9 g
Saturated Fat: 4.7 g   **Trans Fat:** 0.0 g
Cholesterol: 14 mg
Sodium: 20 mg
Potassium: 144 mg
Total Carbohydrates: 6.3 g
Dietary Fibre: 3.3 g   **Sugars:** 0.8 g
Protein: 5.0 g
Vitamin A: 0 %   **Vitamin C:** 0 %,
Calcium: 6 %   **Iron:** 5 %

Ingredients:
- ☐ 1 egg
- ☐ 1/2 teaspoon nutmeg
- ☐ 1/4 cup coconut oil
- ☐ 2 cups whole almonds
- ☐ 2 tablespoons chia seeds
- ☐ 2 tablespoons cinnamon powder
- ☐ 3 tablespoons ginger, freshly grated
- ☐ Dash of salt

☐ Stevia equivalent to 6 tablespoons sugar (9 packets)

Directions:
1. Preheat the oven to 350F or 175C.
2. Blend or food process the chia seeds and the almonds.
3. In a large mixing bowl, mix all the ingredients together.
4. Form into small cookies in a parchment paper lined baking tray.
5. Bake for about 15 minutes at 350F.

Turmeric Ginger Cookies

These cookies are nut-free, dairy-free, flourless, and each cookie is virtually sugar-free. Turmeric and ginger are powerful spices that are widely used for cooking and medicinal purposes. These spices are used to treat various digestion and stomach-related issues. Both spices have antioxidant properties, which help prevent the growth of cancerous tumours

Serves: 15
Prep. Time: 15 minutes
Cook Time: 10-15 minutes

Nutritional Facts

Serving Size: 16 g

Calories: 44
Total Fat: 3.9 g
Saturated Fat: 3.2 g   **Trans Fat:** 0.0 g
Cholesterol: 11 mg
Sodium: 60 mg
Potassium: 50 mg
Total Carbohydrates: 3.6 g
Dietary Fibre: 1.8 g   **Sugars:** 0.7 g
Protein: 0.8 g
Vitamin A: 0 %   **Vitamin C:** 1 %,
Calcium: 0 %   **Iron:** 9 %

Ingredients:

- 1 cup coconut butter, softened
- 1 egg
- 1 teaspoon turmeric powder
- 1 teaspoon vanilla extract
- 1/4 cup low carb granulated sweetener

- ☐ 1/4 teaspoon baking soda
- ☐ 1/4 teaspoon sea salt
- ☐ 1/8 teaspoon black pepper, or more
- ☐ 2 heaping teaspoon ginger, ground

Directions:
1. Place the egg, coconut butter, and vanilla extract into a food processor. Blend until well combined.
2. Add the baking soda, sweetener, and all of the spices. Blend again until combined.
3. Form the cookie mixture into 1-inch balls. Place 1 inch apart in a parchment lined cookie sheet. Press each cookie to flatten into cookie shapes. Do not spread too much.
4. Bake for 350F for about 10-15 minutes or until slightly brown.
5. Allow the cookies to cool down a bit in the cookie sheet. They will be fragile fresh out of the oven. When slightly cool, transfer on a cooling rack and allow to cool completely, hardening as they cool.
6. Store in an airtight container.

Notes:
Do not melt the coconut butter completely, just soften it. If the cookie dough mixture does not form into ball because the butter is too runny, place the mixture in the fridge for a few minutes to make it moldable.

Chocolate Frosted Brownies

These Paleo-friendly and grain-free treats taste just like chocolate cake brownies. If you do not like the subtle flavour of coffee, you can use water. However, coffee does enhance the flavour of chocolate.

Serves: 12-16
Prep. Time: 12 mins
Cook Time: 20 mins

Nutritional Facts
Serving Size: 60 g

Calories: 177
Total Fat: 18.2 g
Saturated Fat: 12.5 g   **Trans Fat:** 0.0 g
Cholesterol: 71 mg
Sodium: 205 mg
Potassium: 107 mg
Total Carbohydrates: 7.8 g
Dietary Fibre: 4.0 g   **Sugars:** 1.1 g
Protein: 2.3 g
Vitamin A: 8 %   **Vitamin C:** 1 %,
Calcium: 1 %   **Iron:** 10 %

Ingredients:
For the brownies:
- ☐ 1/2 cup coconut flour, sifted
- ☐ 3/4 cup low carb sweetener choice
- ☐ 2 tablespoons cocoa powder, (unsweetened)
- ☐ 1/2 cup ghee, butter, or organic red palm oil
- ☐ 1/2 cup brewed coffee or decaf coffee (or 1/2 cup water if you can't have coffee)
- ☐ 1 teaspoon vanilla extract

- ☐ 1 teaspoon baking soda
- ☐ 3 eggs
- ☐ 6 tablespoons coconut milk, unsweetened

For the frosting:
- ☐ 1 1/2 tablespoon coconut milk, unsweetened
- ☐ 1 tablespoon cocoa powder
- ☐ 1/2 cup low carb powdered sweetener
- ☐ 1/2 teaspoon vanilla
- ☐ 1/4 cup ghee, butter, or coconut oil

Directions:
For the brownies:
1. Preheat the oven to 400F.
2. Oil or grease well an 8x8-inch pan. Set aside.
3. In a large ceramic or metal mixing bowl, mix the coconut flour and the sweetener until thoroughly combined. Set aside.
4. In a medium-sized saucepan, combine the ghee, coffee, and cocoa powder. Stir and heat. Bring the mixture to a boil. When boiling, pour into the bowl of coconut mixture. Stir together to combine.
5. Add the eggs, coconut milk, baking soda, and vanilla extract.
6. With an electric mixer or a large spoon, mix until well combined.
7. Pour the batter into the prepared pan.
8. Bake at 400F for 20 minutes or until a toothpick come out clean after inserting it in the center.

For the frosting:
1. In a small saucepan, combine the ghee, cocoa powder, and coconut milk. Stir to mix. Heat and bring to a boil. When boiling, turn the heat to low.

2. Stir the sweetener and the vanilla extract into the saucepan. Mix until the mixture is smooth on very low heat.
3. As soon as you take the brownies out of the oven, pour the warm frosting over the top, covering the entire surface as much as you can. Spread the frosting with a spoon.
4. Allow the brownie and the frosting to completely cool and set. Cut and serve.

Note:

When the brownie and the frosting has cooled enough, you can put it in the fridge to set the frosting faster. I usually cool it on the counter for 15 minutes and then put it in the fridge for about 45 minutes.

Pecan-nutty Almond Butter Coconut Cookies

Satisfy your craving for a sweet treat with these cookies. Although this version is less sweet than the original, these desserts have a crunchy familiar texture. Once you've gotten used to eating less-sugary treats, your taste buds will adjust and you will find these cookies sweet enough.

Serves: 10
Prep. Time: 20 minutes
Cook Time: 12-14 minutes

Nutritional Facts
Serving Size: 38 g

Calories: 174
Total Fat: 16.0 g
Saturated Fat: 4.9 g   **Trans Fat:** 0.0 g
Cholesterol: 0mg
Sodium: 33 mg
Potassium: 165 mg
Total Carbohydrates: 4.7 g
Dietary Fibre: 2.0 g   **Sugars:** 0.9 g
Protein: 4.7 g
Vitamin A: 1 %   **Vitamin C:** 1 %,
Calcium: 4 %   **Iron:** 12 %

Ingredients:
- ☐   2 teaspoons coconut oil, melted
- ☐   2 eggs
- ☐   1/4 cup pecans, chopped
- ☐   1/2 teaspoon vanilla extract

- [ ] 1/2 cup almond butter (sugar-free)
- [ ] 1 teaspoon cinnamon
- [ ] 1 tablespoon coconut flour
- [ ] 1 cup shredded coconut (unsweetened)

Directions:

1. Preheat the oven to 350F.
2. Line a baking sheet with a parchment paper or silicone mat.
3. In a mixing bowl, stir together the coconut oil, eggs, almond butter, and vanilla. This step will take some effort. It will be a little challenging to blend the ingredients together.
4. Slowly stir in the coconut flour and the cinnamon until blended.
5. Add in the shredded coconut and the pecans.
6. In small clumps, scoop a mixture into the prepared baking sheet, making about 8-10 depending on the size you make.
7. With a fork, flatten the clumps into 1/4-inch thick cookies. You may need to coat the fork with extra coconut flour so that it will not stick to the cookies when you flatten them.
8. Bake for about 12-14 minutes. Make sure not to over-bake these so that they will not dry out.

Wal-nutty Coconut Brownies

*Although these brownies are dairy and gluten free,
they are very decadent and rich. They will not taste
anything like coconut. The cocoa will cover the
flavour of coconut. If you want lighter bars, make
sure to use almond flour that is blanched and the
skins removed. The walnuts and the coconut shreds
add a delicious texture.*

Serves: 20
Prep. Time: 15 minutes
Cook Time: 30 minutes

Nutritional Facts
Serving Size: 49 g

Calories: 234
Total Fat: 21.4 g
Saturated Fat: 12.2 g   **Trans Fat:** 0.0 g
Cholesterol: 16 mg
Sodium: 42 mg
Potassium: 226 mg
Total Carbohydrates: 10.6 g
Dietary Fibre: 3.0 g   **Sugars:** 5.6 g
Protein: 4.5 g
Vitamin A: 0 %   **Vitamin C:** 1 %,
Calcium: 4 %   **Iron:** 9 %

Ingredients:
- ☐ 3/4 cup cocoa powder
- ☐ 2 teaspoons stevia powder extract or 1/2 cup organic birch xylitol (or 1/2 cup raw honey or maple syrup)
- ☐ 2 eggs

- ☐ 1/2 teaspoon baking soda
- ☐ 1/2 cup walnuts, chopped
- ☐ 1/2 cup shredded coconut
- ☐ 1/2 cup coconut milk, full- fat, canned
- ☐ 1 teaspoon vanilla extract
- ☐ 1 cup coconut oil, melted
- ☐ 1 cup almond flour, heaping

Directions:
1. Preheat the oven to 350F.
2. In a mixing bowl, combine the eggs, cocoa, coconut milk, coconut oil, and vanilla.
3. In another mixing bowl, combine the baking soda, almond flour, and shredded coconut.
4. Mix the two mixtures together. Pour into a square baking dish.
5. Bake for 30 minutes. When cooked, allow to cool 15 minutes before serving.

Chapter 6: Cakes

Keto Strawberry Dessert

This baked treat is very quick and easy to make. All you will need to do is mix everything together and pop it in the oven and in 5 minutes. This delicious dessert is a very good source of vitamin C. It is also a good source of calcium, vitamin A, protein, and fibre.

Serves: 2
Prep time: 5 minutes
Cook time: 5 minutes

Nutritional Facts
Serving Size: 159 g

Calories: 361
Total Fat: 33.5 g
Saturated Fat: 14.3 g   **Trans Fat**: 0.0g
Cholesterol: 74 mg
Sodium: 42 mg
Potassium: 343 mg
Total Carbohydrates: 12.4 g
Dietary Fibre: 4.4 g   **Sugars**: 4.6 g
Protein: 6.8 g
Vitamin A: 14 %   **Vitamin C**: 71 %,
Calcium: 12 %   **Iron**: 7 %

Ingredients:
- ☐ 1 cup strawberries, chopped
- ☐ ½ cup tablespoons almond powder
- ☐ ½ tablespoon butter
- ☐ 1 cup freshly whipped cream

Directions:
1. Preheat oven at 355 degrees.
2. In a bowl add strawberries, almond powder, and butter and mix well.
3. Transfer into baking dish and bake for 5 minutes.
4. Top with whipped cream and enjoy.

Mexicano Chocolate Cookies

These savory, spicy cookies taste great. They taste delicious that no one would believe they are dairy-free, gluten-free and low-carb. These chocolaty snacks are very rich and have a hint of heat.

Serves: 5
Makes: 15 cookies
Prep. Time: 20 minutes
Cook Time: 15 minutes

Nutrition Facts
Serving Size: 45 g

Calories: 184
Total Fat: 15.1 g
Saturated Fat: 11.8 g   **Trans Fat:** 0 g
Cholesterol: 56 mg
Sodium: 79 mg
Potassium: 111 mg
Total Carbohydrates: 10.3 g
Dietary Fiber: 2.3 g   **Sugar:** 7.4 g
Protein: 2.7 g
Vitamin A: 5%   **Vitamin C:** 2%
Calcium: 2%   **Iron:** 13%
Ingredients:

- 8 tablespoons unsweetened cocoa powder
- 4 large eggs
- 3/4 cup coconut flour
- 3 tablespoons salted butter
- 2 teaspoons vanilla
- 2 1/2 teaspoons cinnamon

- 1/4 teaspoon salt
- 1/2 teaspoons cayenne pepper
- 5 packets of Stevia
- 1/2 cup coconut oil
- 1 1/2 teaspoons chili powder

Directions :

1. Preheat the oven to 350F.
2. Put the coconut flour into a mixing bowl.
3. Add the cocoa powder, cayenne pepper, chili powder, stevia, and salt. Mix all of the ingredients together.
4. In a microwavable container, put the butter and the coconut oil. Microwave for about 10-15 seconds until liquefied.
5. Add the eggs and the vanilla into the butter mixture. Whisk them together.
6. Add the butter mixture into the dry ingredients. Mix well until the dry ingredients are completely soaked with the wet ingredients. Knead together with your hands if you have to.
7. Grease a pan. With your hands, form the dough into cookies. Do not roll because the pieces will crumble.
8. Bake for about 12-15 minutes. The cookies will be soft when you take them out from the oven.
9. Let them cool for a couple of minutes. Enjoy with low-carb milk.

Chocolate Cupcakes

Mascarpone cheese is similar to cream cheese in both texture and taste. This cheese is often used in Italian desserts for its mild creamy taste. The cheese also makes these cupcakes ultra-creamy!

Serves: 12
Prep time: 10 minutes
Cook time: 15 minutes

Nutritional Facts
Serving Size: 24 g

Calories: 65
Total Fat: 3.8 g
Saturated Fat: 0.9 g   **Trans Fat:** 0.0g
Cholesterol: 30 mg
Sodium: 24 mg
Potassium: 77 mg
Total Carbohydrates: 3.2 g
Dietary Fibre: 1.7 g   **Sugars:** 6.8 g
Protein: 6.8 g
Vitamin A: 1 %   **Vitamin C:** 0 %,
Calcium: 3 %   **Iron:** 4 %

Ingredients:

- [ ] 2 eggs
- [ ] ½ cup protein powder
- [ ] ½ cup almond powder
- [ ] 2 oz. mascarpone
- [ ] ¼ cup dark cocoa powder
- [ ] 1 tablespoon flaxseed, ground
- [ ] ¼ cup liquid sweetener

Directions:
1. In a bowl add eggs and beat until smooth.
2. Add protein powder, almond powder, cocoa powder, liquid sweetener, mascarpone and beat for 1-2 minutes.
3. Pour this mixture into cupcakes mold and bake for 15 minutes.
4. Serve and enjoy.

No-Bake Mini Lemon Tarts

These sugar-free, egg-free, and gluten-free tarts are little, tasty treats. They are packed with good fats, and if you use coconut oil, they are also dairy-free. You can also opt to use nut meal instead of nut flour. The nut meal will make the crust look brown.

Serves: 24
Prep. Time: 30 minutes
Cook Time: 0 minutes

Nutritional Facts
Serving Size: 30 g

Calories: 128
Total Fat: 12.4 g
Saturated Fat: 5.7 g   **Trans Fat:** 0.0 g
Cholesterol: 16 mg
Sodium: 76 mg
Potassium: 96 mg
Total Carbohydrates: 3.7 g
Dietary Fibre: 1.9 g   **Sugars:** 0.9 g
Protein: 2.3 g
Vitamin A: 4 %   **Vitamin C:** 4 %,
Calcium: 3 %   **Iron:** 4 %

Ingredients:
For the crust:

- ☐ 4 1/2 tablespoons butter, coconut oil, or ghee, melted
- ☐ 3/4 cup coconut, dried, finely grated,
- ☐ 3 tablespoons lemon juice
- ☐ Low carb sweetener equivalent to 2 tablespoons sugar

- 1 cup almond, or other nut flour like cashew
- 1 1/2 teaspoons vanilla extract
- Pinch of salt

For the filling:
- 1 teaspoon vanilla extract, sugar-free
- 1/2 cup butter, coconut oil, or ghee, softened to room temperature
- 1/3 cup coconut, full fat (or other low-carb milk like almond)
- 1/3 cup fresh lemon juice
- 1/4 teaspoon salt
- 2 teaspoons lemon extract
- Grated zest from 2 medium lemons
- Low carb sweetener equivalent to1/4 cup plus 1 tablespoon sugar

Directions:
For the crust:
1. Grease 2 pieces of 12-cup size mini-muffin pans.
2. In a medium mixing bowl, combine all of the crust ingredients until well mixed.
3. Roll 2 teaspoons of the crust dough mixture into balls and then press into the prepared tart pans.
4. Chill the crusts until ready to fill.

For the filling:
1. Put the butter in a bowl. Beat until fluffy. Alternatively, you can blend it in a food processor.
2. Add the milk, sweetener, lemon juice, extracts, salt, and zest into the bowl. Beat until the mixture is soft. If using processor, then blend until smooth.
3. Taste test. Add more sweetener or lemon juice as needed.

To assemble the tarts:
1. Spoon the filling into the assembled crusts. If desired, garnish with melon zest.
2. Refrigerate until the filling is set.

Notes:
If you have leftover filling, serve it as is as lemon pudding. Alternatively, you can put them in mini paper cup cake liners or muffin pans, freeze, and then serve as lemon fat bombs.

Slow Cooker Chocolate Cake

Put your slow cooker to use with this delicious dark chocolate cake. For more fat, substitute coconut milk with full table cream.

Serves: 10
Slow Cooker: 6-quart
Prep. Time: 20 minutes
Cook Time: Low for 2 1/2-3 hours

Nutritional Facts
Serving Size: 83 g

Calories: 330
Total Fat: 28.6 g
Saturated Fat: 12.9 g   **Trans. Fat:** 0 g
Cholesterol: 111 mg
Sodium: 167 mg
Potassium: 524 mg
Total Carbohydrates: 11.6 g
Dietary Fiber: 5.9 g   **Sugar:** 2.4 g
Protein: 12.8 g
Vitamin A: 8%   **Vitamin C:** 2%
Calcium: 14%   **Iron:** 26%

Ingredients:
- ☐ 4 large eggs
- ☐ 3/4 cup sweetener of choice
- ☐ 3/4 cup almond or coconut milk, unsweetened
- ☐ 2/3 cup cocoa powder

- [ ] 2 teaspoons baking powder
- [ ] 1/4 teaspoon salt
- [ ] 1/4 cup whey protein powder, unflavored
- [ ] 1/2 cup butter, melted
- [ ] 1 teaspoon vanilla extract
- [ ] 1 1/2 cups almond flour

Optional:
- [ ] 1/2 cup chocolate chips, sugar-free

Directions:
1. Grease the slow cooker.
2. In a medium mixing bowl, whisk the almond flour, baking powder, cocoa powder, protein powder, sweetener, and salt together.
3. Stir in the milk, eggs, butter, and vanilla extract. Stir until well combined. Stir in the chocolate chips, if using.
4. Pour into the greased slow cooker. Cook for 2 1/2-3 hours on low. Turn off the slow cooker. Let cool for 20-30 minutes. When cooled to a warm, cut into slices. Serve lightly topped with whipped cream.

Slow Cooker Pecan-Pumpkin Pie Cake

A delicious fall treat that you can have all year around. If you have a programmable slow cooker you can make this the night before so when you wake up you have a deliciously warm fat bomb you can eat in the morning.

Serves: 10
Slow Cooker: 6-quart
Prep. Time: 30 minutes
Cook Time: Low for 2 1/2 -3 hours

Nutritional Facts

Serving Size: 67 g

Calories: 134
Total Fat: 9.9 g
Saturated Fat: 6.3 g   **Trans. Fat:** 0 g
Cholesterol: 98 mg
Sodium: 133 mg
Potassium: 247 mg
Total Carbohydrates: 5.1 g
Dietary Fiber: 1.7 g   **Sugar:** 1.7 g
Protein: 7.2 g
Vitamin A: 81%   **Vitamin C:** 3%
Calcium: 8%   **Iron:** 12%

Ingredients:

- ☐ 4 large eggs

- [ ] 3/4 cup Swerve Sweetener
- [ ] 2 teaspoon baking powder
- [ ] 1/4 teaspoon salt
- [ ] 1/4 teaspoon ground cloves
- [ ] 1/4 cup whey protein powder, unflavored
- [ ] 1/4 cup butter, melted
- [ ] 1/3 cup coconut flour
- [ ] 1 teaspoon vanilla extract
- [ ] 1 teaspoon ground ginger
- [ ] 1 cup pumpkin puree
- [ ] 1 1/2 teaspoon ground cinnamon
- [ ] 1 1/2 cups raw pecans

Directions:
1. Grease the slow cooker or line with parchment paper.
2. Put the pecans in a high-powered blender. Process the pecans until ground into coarse meal. Make sure not to turn them into butter. Transfer into a large mixing bowl.
3. Into the bowl with pecan meal, whisk in the coconut flour, baking powder, sweetener, protein powder, ginger, cloves, cinnamon, and salt.
4. Stir in the eggs, pumpkin puree, butter, and the vanilla. Stir until well combined.
5. Spread the mix into the greased slow cooker. Cook for 2 1/2 -3 hours on low or until set and the top is firm to the touch.

Lemon Blueberry Mug Cake

These cakes are dairy-free and nut-free. The juicy blueberry taste burst deliciously through the flavour of the tart lemon.

Serves: 5
Prep. Time: 20 minutes
Cook Time: 10 minutes

Nutritional Facts
Serving Size: 136 g

Calories: 303
Total Fat: 28.6 g
Saturated Fat: 22.7 g   **Trans Fat:** 0.0 g
Cholesterol: 149 mg
Sodium: 347 mg
Potassium: 229 mg
Total Carbohydrates: 20.5 g
Dietary Fibre: 9.3 g   **Sugars:** 4.4 g
Protein: 6.6 g
Vitamin A: 4 %   **Vitamin C:** 18 %,
Calcium: 3 %   **Iron:** 26 %

Ingredients:
- ☐ 1 teaspoon baking soda
- ☐ 1/2 cup coconut milk
- ☐ 1/2 cup frozen wild blueberries
- ☐ 1/2 cup plus 1 teaspoon coconut flour, divided
- ☐ 1/2 teaspoon lemon extract
- ☐ 1/4 cup coconut oil (could also use avocado oil here), melted

- ☐ 1/4 cup Swerve Sweetener or any low carb sweetener
- ☐ 1/4 teaspoon stevia extract (or equivalent stevia powder)
- ☐ 4 large eggs
- ☐ Pinch salt
- ☐ Zest of 1 lemon

Directions:

1. In a medium mixing bowl, whisk the 1/2 cup coconut flour, baking soda, lemon zest, sweetener, and salt together.
2. Stir in the coconut milk, coconut oil, eggs, stevia extract, and lemon extract.
3. In a small mixing bowl, toss the 1 teaspoon coconut flour and blueberries. Add the coconut flour tossed berries into the batter. Mix gently.
4. Divide the batter between 5 mugs.
5. Cook each mug on high in the microwave for about 1 minute and 30seconds. You can cook it longer, if desired.

Molten Lava Chocolate Cakes

This cake is fudgy with a molten gooey centre. This low carb and dairy free version is also high in iron and a good source of protein.

Serves: 2
Prep. Time: 20 minutes
Cook Time: 11-12 minutes

Nutritional Facts
Serving Size: 123 g

Calories: 527
Total Fat: 54.3 g
Saturated Fat: 36.9 g   **Trans Fat:** 0.0 g
Cholesterol: 186 mg
Sodium: 79 mg
Potassium: 414 mg
Total Carbohydrates: 15.6 g
Dietary Fibre: 8.3 g   **Sugars:** 1.1 g
Protein: 12.4 g
Vitamin A: 5 %   **Vitamin C:** 0 %,
Calcium: 8 %   **Iron:** 41 %

Ingredients:
- 1 tablespoon almond flour
- 1/4 cup coconut oil, plus more for greasing the ramekins)
- 1/4 teaspoon vanilla extract
- 2 1/5 ounces dark chocolate, dairy free (85%)
- 2 large eggs
- 2 tablespoons equivalent sweetener (3 packets)
- Cocoa powder, for dusting

Directions:
1. Preheat oven 375F.
2. Grease 2 pieces 4-ounce ramekins with the coconut oil and then dust with the cocoa powder.
3. Melt the coconut oil and the chocolate together, and then add the vanilla extract.
4. In a large mixing bowl, whisk the eggs and the sweetener together.
5. Slowly add the chocolate mixture into the egg mixture. Beat until well combined.
6. Add almond flour into the bowl. Mix until well incorporated.
7. Divide the batter into the 2 ramekins.
8. Bake for about11-12 minutes. Make sure that you do not over bake.
9. Run a knife along the edges of the ramekins. Cover the ramekin with a plate. Flip the ramekin over together with the plate. Lift the ramekin, dislodging the cake into the plate.
10. Repeat with the other ramekin. Serve immediately.

Chapter 7: Fudge

Sugar-Free Fudge

This low carb, completely sugar-free fudge will remind you of milk chocolate. If you want a darker chocolate taste, just add more cocoa powder.

Serves: 12
Prep. Time: 21 minutes, plus 15 minutes freezing
Cook Time: 0 minutes

Nutritional Facts
Serving Size: 27 g

Calories: 174
Total Fat: 19.6 g
Saturated Fat: 16.9 g   **Trans Fat:** 0.0 g
Cholesterol: 0 mg
Sodium: 79 mg
Potassium: 59 mg
Total Carbohydrates: 2.3 g
Dietary Fibre: 1.1 g   **Sugars:** 0 g
Protein: 0.4 g
Vitamin A: 0 %   **Vitamin C:** 0 %,
Calcium: 0 %   **Iron:** 2 %

Ingredients:
- [ ] 1 cup coconut oil, soft yet still solid
- [ ] 1 teaspoon vanilla extract
- [ ] 1/2 teaspoon almond extract
- [ ] 1/2 teaspoon sea salt
- [ ] 1/4 cup cocoa powder
- [ ] 1/4 cup coconut milk, full fat

☐ 1/4 cup Swerve confectioners (or a drop of stevia)

Directions:

1. Put the coconut milk and oil in a medium mixing bowl. With a hand or a stand mixer, mix on high speed until the mixture is well combined and glossy.
2. Add the remaining ingredients into the bowl.
3. On low speed, stir with the mixer until the mixture is combined.
4. Increase the speed. Continue mixing until the mixture is well combined.
5. Taste the fudge. Adjust to your desired sweetness.
6. Line a loaf pan with wax or parchment paper. Pour the fudge mixture into the loaf pan. Place the loaf fan in the fridge for at least 15 minutes, until the fudge is set.
7. Use the edge of the wax or parchment paper to pull the fudge from the pan.
8. Place on a cutting board. Cut into 12 equal-sized squares.
9. Store in an airtight container and keep in the freezer.

Coconut Chocolate Almond Fudge

This fudge is a delicious dessert that is absolutely sugar-free. These sweet treats are very easy to make, too. Just dump everything in toba high-powered blender and your good to freeze!

Serves: 8
Makes: 16 squares
Serving Size: 2 squares
Prep Time: 5 minutes, plus 1 hour freezing
Cook Time: 0 minutes

Nutritional Facts
Serving Size: 16 g

Calories: 80
Total Fat: 8.6 g
Saturated Fat: 7.4 g   **Trans Fat:** 0.0 g
Cholesterol: 0 mg
Sodium: 1 mg
Potassium: 57 mg
Total Carbohydrates: 2.7 g
Dietary Fibre: 1.5 g   **Sugars:** 0.0 g
Protein: 0.7 g
Vitamin A: 0 %   **Vitamin C:** 0 %,
Calcium: 0 %   **Iron:** 4 %

Ingredients:
- [ ] 1 teaspoon vanilla extract, sugar-free
- [ ] 1/2 cup cocoa powder, unsweetened
- [ ] 1/2 cup coconut oil, softened
- [ ] 1/3 cup coconut flakes, unsweetened
- [ ] 1/4 cup almond milk

☐ 1/4 cup low carb sweetener

Directions:
1. Combine all of the ingredients in a blender or a food processor.
2. Blend until everything is well combined.
3. In a parchment paper lined square or rectangle container.
4. Refrigerate until the mixture is hard.
5. When hard, remove from container. Cut into 16 squares.

Naturally-Colored Fudge

Are you looking for a sweet treat that's low in sugar, and not loaded with artificial colouring and fructose? Then this is the fudge you've have been looking for! You can make these fudges coloured purple, green, or pink..

Serves: 12
Prep. Time: 5 minutes, plus 1 hour freezing
Cook Time: 5 minutes

Nutritional Facts
Serving Size: 55 g

Calories: 407
Total Fat: 44.2 g
Saturated Fat: 32.0 g   **Trans Fat:** 0.0 g
Cholesterol: 0 mg
Sodium: 51 mg
Potassium: 117 mg
Total Carbohydrates: 5.5 g
Dietary Fibre: 3.0 g   **Sugars:** 0.8 g
Protein: 3.4 g
Vitamin A: 0 %   **Vitamin C:** 0 %,
Calcium: 4 %   **Iron:** 3 %

Ingredients:
- ☐ 2 cups coconut oil
- ☐ 1 cup nut or seed butter
- ☐ 1/2 cup low carb sweetener
- ☐ 2 teaspoons vanilla
- ☐ 1/4 t salt

For the green fudge:
- ☐ 1/2 cup dried parsley flakes

For the purple fudge:
- ☐ 3/4 cup blueberries

For the red/pink fudge:
- ☐ 1 cup finely chopped beets (beet powder is an easier addition)

Directions:
1. In a small saucepan, melt the coconut oil.
2. When melted, pour into the blender. Add the remaining of the ingredients and the ingredient of the color you want your candies to be. Blend until the mixture is smooth.
3. Pour the mixture into an 8x8-inch pan. You can choose larger pans. This will make thinner fudge.
4. Freeze the mixture until solid. Cut into squares.

Notes:
If you have a high-powered blender, like Vitamix, there is no need to melt the coconut oil. Just put all of the ingredients in the blender and puree until smooth.

If you make form this fudge thin enough, you can cut them out using cookie cutters.

Mint Fudge

This healthy dessert is naturally coloured green by the parsley. You will not taste any hint of parsley in this sweet treat. The minty taste also adds a delicious cool flavour into the fudge.

Serves: 12
Prep. Time: 5 minutes, plus 1 hour freezing time
Cook Time: 10 minutes

Nutritional Facts
Serving Size: 48 g

Calories: 323
Total Fat: 33.6 g
Saturated Fat: 21.0g   **Trans Fat:** 0.0 g
Cholesterol: 0 mg
Sodium: 44 mg
Potassium: 162 mg
Total Carbohydrates: 6.3 g
Dietary Fibre: 3.5 g   **Sugars:** 1.0 g
Protein: 4.4 g
Vitamin A: 4 %   **Vitamin C:** 5 %,
Calcium: 6 %   **Iron:** 5 %

Ingredients:
- [ ] 2 teaspoons vanilla
- [ ] 1/4 teaspoon salt
- [ ] 1/2 cup sweetener
- [ ] 1/2 cup or more dried parsley flakes
- [ ] 1 teaspoon peppermint extract
- [ ] 1 1/5 cups nut butter (you can also use seed butter)
- [ ] 1 1/2 cups coconut oil

☐ Melted chocolate

Directions:
1. In a small saucepan, melt the coconut oil.
2. Put the remaining of the ingredients in a blender. Add the coconut oil. Blend the mixture until smooth.
3. Pour the mixture into an 8x8-inch pan.
4. Freeze until solid.
5. Store in the refrigerator.

Notes:
If using a high-powered blender. Just blend everything until smooth. If you want a lighter seed or nut mix, use only 3/4 cup of nut or seed butter.

Almond Butter Coconut Fudge

This fat bomb is absolutely sugar-free. Using almond milk also makes them dairy-free.

Serves: 12 servings
Prep. Time: 5 minutes, 2-3 hours freezing
Cook Time: 0 minutes

Nutritional Facts
Serving Size: 46 g

Calories: 301
Total Fat: 31.1 g
Saturated Fat: 17.9 g   **Trans Fat:** 0.0 g
Cholesterol: 0 mg
Sodium: 1 mg
Potassium: 172 mg
Total Carbohydrates: 6.0 g
Dietary Fibre: 1.9 g   **Sugars:** 0.0 g
Protein: 4.5 g
Vitamin A: 0 %   **Vitamin C:** 0 %,
Calcium: 6 %   **Iron:** 5 %

Ingredients:
- [ ] 1 cup coconut oil
- [ ] 1 cup unsweetened almond butter
- [ ] 1 teaspoon vanilla extract
- [ ] 1/4 cup coconut milk
- [ ] Stevia to taste

Directions:
1. Melt the coconut oil and the almond butter until soft.

2. Blend all the ingredients together until well combined.
3. Pour the mixture into a baking pan.
4. Refrigerate for about 2-3 hours or until the fudge is set.
5. When frozen, cut into chunks.

One Skillet Pepperoni Pizza

The perfect recipe for when your craving the ooey gooey taste of a pepperoni pizza. For crunchy goodnesss add crumbled bacon after pizza is removed from the oven.

Serves: 4
Prep. Time: 10 minutes
Cook Time: 20 minutes

Nutrition Facts
Serving Size: 62 g

Calories: 196
Total Fat: 14.3 g
Saturated Fat: 6.6 g   **Trans Fat:** 0.3 g
Cholesterol: 38 mg
Sodium: 526 mg
Potassium: 64 mg
Total Carbohydrates: 2.8 g
Dietary Fiber: 0 g   **Sugar:** 0.8 g
Protein: 14.5 g
Vitamin A: 11%   **Vitamin C:** 2%
Calcium: 27%   **Iron:** 3%

Ingredients:

- 4 ounces mozzarella cheese, or more to cover the bottom of 10-inch skillet
- 12 pepperoni slices
- 1 ounce Parmesan cheese
- 2 tablespoons tomatoes, crushed

- ☐ 1 teaspoon garlic powder
- ☐ 1 teaspoon Italian seasoning or dried basil
- ☐ 1 teaspoon red pepper, crushed
- ☐ 1 teaspoon basil, fresh, torn

Directions:
1. Heat a small, non-stick skillet over medium heat.
2. Evenly cover the bottom with the mozzarella cheese. This will serve as the crust.
3. With the back of a spoon, lightly spread the tomatoes over the cheese, leaving a border around the edges of the cheese crust.
4. Sprinkle with the garlic powder and the Italian seasoning or dried basil.
5. Arrange the pepperoni on top. Cook until bubbled, sizzling, and the edges of the crust are brown.
6. With a spatula, try lifting the edges. When done, the pizza will lift easily from the pan. If the pizza still sticks, it means it is not yet done. Lift and check frequently.
7. When the pizza lifts up easily, work the spatula slowly and gently underneath, loosening up the entire pizza. Transfer to a cutting board.
8. Lightly sprinkle with parmesan, basil leaves, and red pepper.
9. Cool for about 5 minutes to cool and allow the crust to firm. Cut with a pizza cutter. Transfer to a serving plate.

Lemon Curd

Are you craving for some lemon curd? Then this version will thrill you. Enjoy this recipe with a dollop of sliced berries on top, or use it as a filling for another recipe.

Serves: 2
Prep. Time: 5 minutes
Cook Time: 10 minutes

Nutritional Facts
Serving Size: 174 g

Calories: 445
Total Fat: 44.5g
Saturated Fat: 25.5 g   **Trans Fat:** 0.0 g
Cholesterol: 487 mg
Sodium: 336 mg
Potassium: 171 mg
Total Carbohydrates: 6.3 g
Dietary Fibre: 2.2 g   **Sugars:** 1.8 g
Protein: 9.8 g
Vitamin A: 31 %   **Vitamin C:** 47 %,
Calcium: 6 %   **Iron:** 8 %

Ingredients:
- ☐ 6 tablespoons butter, cut in to cubes
- ☐ 2 tablespoons + 2 teaspoon Swerve* or equivalent low carb sweetener
- ☐ 2 large eggs
- ☐ 2 large egg yolks
- ☐ 1/2 cup lemon juice

Directions:

1. In a saucepan, whisk the eggs, yolks, sweetener, and lemon juice together.
2. Add the butter. Continuously stirring to mix, turn the heat on to very low. Remember, that there are eggs. Too much heat will make the mixture into a lemony scramble.
3. Once the butter has melted, then you can turn the heat up to medium-high.
4. Stir continuously until the mixture thickens. The curd is cooked when the consistency is like conditioner.
5. Remove the saucepan from the heat. Pour the mixture through a mesh strainer to remove any egg bits.
6. Store in the fridge.

Notes:

Meyer lemons have more natural sweetness. If you are using regular lemons, you will need to add more sweeteners.

Crustless Pumpkin Pie

Each serving is packed with tons of vitamin A. Every bite is moist and absolutely delicious. Plus, you do not have to do any complicated method to make it, all you have to do is mix, pour, and bake.

Serves: 6
Prep time: 5 minutes
Cook time: 15 minutes

Nutritional Facts
Serving Size: 96 g

Calories: 140
Total Fat: 11.6 g
Saturated Fat: 6.8 g   **Trans Fat:** 0.0g
Cholesterol: 83 mg
Sodium: 90 mg
Potassium: 152 mg
Total Carbohydrates: 7.2 g
Dietary Fibre: 2.5 g   **Sugars:** 3.2 g
Protein: 3.0 g
Vitamin A: 135 %   **Vitamin C:** 12 %,
Calcium: 4 %   **Iron:** 6 %

Ingredients:
- 1 cup pumpkin puree
- 1 cup cream
- 1 cup raspberries
- 2 eggs
- ½ teaspoon vanilla extract
- ¼ cup butter

Directions:
1. Preheat oven at 355 degrees.
2. In a bowl add eggs and beat until smooth.
3. Add butter, pumpkin puree, cream, vanilla extract and beat for 1 minute.
4. Transfer into baking dish and bake for 15 minutes.
5. Serve and enjoy.

Peppermint Patties

Store-bought versions of these sweet treats contain artificial flavours, corn syrup, and mysterious ingredients. These homemade desserts are healthier and you probably already have all the ingredients to make them at home. With the refreshing flavour of mint, these creamy, smooth patties are as delicious as the store-bought ones.

Serves: 6
Prep. Time: 20 minutes
Cook Time: 0 minutes

Nutritional Facts

Serving Size: 32 g

Calories: 146
Total Fat: 14.8 g
Saturated Fat: 12.9 g   **Trans Fat:** 0.0 g
Cholesterol: 0 mg
Sodium: 5 mg
Potassium: 129 mg
Total Carbohydrates: 4.6 g
Dietary Fibre: 2.6 g   **Sugars:** 1.5 g
Protein: 1.1 g
Vitamin A: 0 %   **Vitamin C:** 2 %,
Calcium: 0 %   **Iron:** 20 %

Ingredients:

- ☐ 3/4 cup coconut butter, melted
- ☐ 3 tablespoons coconut oil, melted
- ☐ 1-2 tablespoons cacao powder or more, depending on how chocolatey you want them
- ☐ 1/4 cup coconut, finely shredded

☐　1/2 teaspoon peppermint extract, pure

Directions:
1. Mix 1 tablespoon of the coconut oil, shredded coconut, coconut butter, and peppermint extract until well combined.
2. Pour the mixture into mini muffin tins, filling them 1/2 full.
3. Place in the refrigerator for about 15 minutes or until hard.
4. Mix the cacao powder and the remaining 2 tablespoons coconut oil. Add more cacao if you want a chocolatier taste.
5. Pour the mixture over the coconut butter mixture, filling the muffin tins.
6. Return to the refrigerator. Freeze until the chocolate is set.
7. When ready to enjoy, just soften the cups in the counter for about 5 minutes and eat.
8. Store in airtight container and keep in the refrigerator.

Orange Butter Pecan Sandwiches

With a creamy filling, these toasted pecan sandwiches are a delight and are simple and fast to make. The filling adds an orange kick that will keep you coming back for more.

Serves: 2
Prep. Time: 10 minutes
Cook Time: 8-10 minutes

Nutritional Facts
Serving Size: 21 g

Calories: 82
Total Fat: 8.2 g
Saturated Fat: 4.1 g   **Trans Fat:** 0.0 g
Cholesterol: 18 mg
Sodium: 194 mg
Potassium: 30 mg
Total Carbohydrates: 1.0 g
Dietary Fibre: 0.0 g   **Sugars:** 0.6 g
Protein: 1.7 g
Vitamin A: 5 %   **Vitamin C:** 1 %,
Calcium: 1 %   **Iron:** 1 %

Ingredients:
- ☐ 4 pecan halves
- ☐ 1/2 tablespoon unsalted butter
- ☐ 1 ounce Neufchatel cheese
- ☐ 1/2 teaspoon orange zest, finely grated
- ☐ Pinch sea salt

Directions:

1. Toast the pecans for about 8-10 minutes at 350F in the oven. Set aside. Allow to cool.
2. Soften the cream cheese and butter.
3. Add the orange zest.
4. Mix well until creamy and smooth.
5. Spread the mixture between two pecan halves. Sprinkle with sea salt. Enjoy!

Salt and Roasted Rosemary Almonds

These sweet and salty almonds are great to take with you when you're on the go. Quick and easy to make, you can make a whole month's worth in less than 30 minutes.

Serves: 4
Prep. Time: 5 minutes
Cook Time: 15 minutes

Nutrition Facts
Serving Size: 55 g

Calories: 309
Total Fat: 27.2 g
Saturated Fat: 3.9 g   **Trans Fat:** 0 g
Cholesterol: 8 mg
Sodium: 1164 m g
Potassium: 366 mg
Total Carbohydrates: 11.3 g
Dietary Fiber: 6.7 g   **Sugar:** 2 g
Protein: 10.2 g
Vitamin A: 3%   **Vitamin C:** 2%
Calcium: 15%   **Iron:** 13%

Ingredients:
- [ ] 2 cups whole almonds, raw, skin-on
- [ ] 2 tablespoons dried rosemary
- [ ] 1 tablespoon ghee
- [ ] 1/4 teaspoon black pepper, freshly ground
- [ ] 2 teaspoons kosher salt

Directions:
1. In a large skillet over medium-low heat, melt the ghee.
2. Put in the nuts, arranging them in a single layer in the skillet. Stir the almonds, coating each with the ghee.
3. Add in the rosemary, salt, and pepper. Taste and adjust seasoning according to taste..
4. Toast the almonds for about 8-12 minutes, stirring often, until aromatic and darkened.
5. Transfer to a plate. Allow to cool to room temperature. Serve or store in an airtight container for up to 7 days.

Watermelon Cream Soup

This refreshing soup is easy to make and perfect for those hot days of summer. Each serving is packed with vitamin A, vitamin C, and calcium. You can even keep them chilled and garnish with some sliced strawberries on top of the whipped cream before serving.

Serves: 2
Prep time: 10 minutes
Cook time: 15 minutes

Nutritional Facts
Serving Size: 170 g

Calories: 231
Total Fat: 21.2 g
Saturated Fat: 13.2 g   **Trans Fat:** 0.0g
Cholesterol: 72 mg
Sodium: 319 mg
Potassium: 195 mg
Total Carbohydrates: 9.5 g
Dietary Fibre: 0.7 g   **Sugars:** 5.7 g
Protein: 2.3 g
Vitamin A: 23 %   **Vitamin C:** 31 %,
Calcium: 7 %   **Iron:** 2 %

Ingredients:
- [ ] 1 cup seeded watermelon chunks
- [ ] ¼ cup strawberries
- [ ] 2 tablespoons organic sour cream
- [ ] 1 teaspoon lemon juice
- [ ] 1 teaspoon chopped mint leaves
- [ ] 1 cup freshly whipped cream

☐ ¼ teaspoon salt

Directions:
1. In a blender, add watermelon, strawberries, salt, lemon juice, sour cream, mint and blend until smooth.
2. Transfer into serving dish and top with whipped cream.
3. Serve and enjoy.

Bacon and Cheese Jalapeno Popper

I have only recently discovered these delicious poppers and feel robbed of all the years I could have enjoyed them. These poppers are so tasty that I have eaten them every day for about a week and still want more!

Serves: 1
Prep. Time: 30 minutes
Cook Time: 10 minutes

Nutrition Facts
Serving Size: 158 g

Calories: 614
Total Fat: 53.6 g
Saturated Fat: 26.5 g   **Trans Fat:** 0 g
Cholesterol: 156mg
Sodium: 1725 mg
Potassium: 472 mg
Total Carbohydrates: 5 g
Dietary Fiber: 0.5 g   **Sugar:** 1 g
Protein: 27.9 g
Vitamin A: 27%   **Vitamin C:** 12%
Calcium: 8%   **Iron:** 11%

Ingredients:

- 3 slices bacon
- 3 ounces cream cheese
- 1/4 teaspoon onion powder

- 1/4 teaspoon garlic powder
- 1/2 teaspoon dried parsley
- 1 piece medium jalapeno pepper
- Salt and pepper, to taste

Directions :

1. In a pan, fry the slices of bacon until crisp. Remove the bacon from the pan, keeping the bacon grease for later use. Allow the bacon to cool.
2. De-seed the jalapeno pepper and then dice into small pieces.
3. In a mixing bowl, combine the jalapeno, cream cheese, and spices, seasoning with salt and pepper to taste.
4. Add the bacon fat into the cream cheese. Mix together until a solid mixture is formed.
5. Crumble the crispy bacon and put in a plate.
6. With your hands, roll the cream cheese into balls and then roll each ball into the crumbled bacon.

Hot Cross Chocolate Buns

This traditional sweet treat is usually served on Good Friday, but they are so good you'll want to eat it year round!

Serves: 8
Prep. Time: 10 minutes
Cook Time: 15-17 minutes

Nutritional Facts
Serving Size: 83 g

Calories: 192
Total Fat: 16.3 g
Saturated Fat: 12.8 g   **Trans Fat:** 0.0 g
Cholesterol: 83 mg
Sodium: 131 mg
Potassium: 247 mg
Total Carbohydrates: 8.5 g
Dietary Fibre: 2.8 g   **Sugars:** 4.9 g
Protein: 5.7 g
Vitamin A: 2 %   **Vitamin C:** 3 %,
Calcium: 3 %   **Iron:** 19 %

Ingredients:
For the buns:
- [ ] 4 eggs
- [ ] 3 tablespoons cacao powder
- [ ] 1/4 cup cacao nibs
- [ ] 1/3 cup + 2 tablespoons coconut flour
- [ ] 1/2 teaspoon baking soda
- [ ] 1 cup coconut milk

For the crosses:
2 egg whites
1 plus 1/2 tablespoons coconut flour

For greasing:
Coconut oil

Directions:
For the buns:
1. Preheat the oven to 340F or 170C.
2. Grease 8 pieces muffin tins with coconut oil.
3. With an electric beater, beat the eggs for about 1 minute.
4. Add the coconut milk. Beat again.
5. Add the baking soda, coconut flour, and cocoa powder. Mix again with the electric beater for another 1 minute.
6. Scoop the batter into muffin tins. Set aside.

For the crosses:
1. With an electric beater, mix the egg whites.
2. Add the coconut flour. Beat again.
3. Scoop the egg mixture into a plastic bag.
4. Snip of the corner of the plastic bag and then pipe the egg white mixture on top of the buns, making crosses.
5. Bake the buns for about 15-17 minutes.

4-Ingredient Homemade Nutella

This 4-ingredient, simple, homemade version of Nutella is gluten-free and vegan friendly. Also a perfect topping for pancakes, baked goods, fruits, waffles, and more.

Serves: 2 cups (about 32 tablespoons)
Serving Size: 2 tablespoons
Prep Time: 15 minutes
Cook Time: 15 minutes

Nutritional Facts

Serving Size: 32 g

Calories: 194
Total Fat: 18.9 g
Saturated Fat: 3.1 g   **Trans Fat:** 0.0 g
Cholesterol: 0 mg
Sodium: 60 mg
Potassium: 227 mg
Total Carbohydrates: 6.2 g
Dietary Fibre: 3.5 g   **Sugars:** 1.2 g
Protein: 4.7 g
Vitamin A: 0 %   **Vitamin C:** 3 %,
Calcium: 4 %   **Iron:** 13 %

Ingredients:

- ☐ 3 cups hazelnuts, roasted or raw, unsalted
- ☐ 2/3 cup or 3.4 ounces dark chocolate, dairy-free, chopped or 3 tablespoons unsweetened cocoa powder or cacao powder
- ☐ 1/2 teaspoon sea salt
- ☐ 1 teaspoon pure vanilla extract

Directions:

1. Preheat the oven to 350F.
2. Put the hazel nuts in a baking sheet, arranging them in a single layer.
3. If using raw nuts, roast for about 12-15 minutes. If using roasted nuts, heat for about 8-10 minutes to loosen the skin and warm the natural oils. This will make it to blend into butter.
4. Remove from the oven. Allow to cool slightly. Transfer into a large kitchen towel. Using your hands, roll the nuts to remove the skin. Get as much skin off, but it does not have to be perfect.
5. Put the hazel nuts into a high-speed blender or a food processor. Blend on low for about 8-10 minutes or until the nuts turn to butter. Scrape down the sides when needed.
6. Meanwhile, heat the chocolate for 30 seconds in the microwave or over a double boiler. Set aside.
7. When the hazelnut is smooth and creamy, add the melted chocolate, vanilla, and sea salt. Blend or puree again until the mixture is well incorporated.
8. Taste test and adjust the seasonings as needed, adding more vanilla or salt, if desired.
9. Transfer your Nutella into a clean jar. Store at room temperature for about 2-3 weeks or more.

Notes:

If your Nutella mixture is not sweet enough, you can add 1-2 tablespoons of agave or maple syrup. However, the more liquid sweetener you add, the stiffer or firmer your Nutella will become.

If using 3 tablespoons unsweetened cocoa powder or cacao powder, add following step number 7 and on.

Chocolate and Coconut Macaroons

What I love about this recipe is that I can make good old macaroons and chocolate flavoured treats in one setting. These macaroons are high in iron.

Serves: 10
Prep. Time: 20 minutes
Cook Time: 12-15 minutes

Nutritional Facts

Serving Size: 57 g

Calories: 181
Total Fat: 17.9 g
Saturated Fat: 14.8 g   **Trans Fat:** 0.0 g
Cholesterol: 49 mg
Sodium: 24 mg
Potassium: 175 mg
Total Carbohydrates: 5.5 g
Dietary Fibre: 3.1 g   **Sugars:** 1.6 g
Protein: 3.0 g
Vitamin A: 1 %   **Vitamin C:** 2 %,
Calcium: 1 %   **Iron:** 23 %

Ingredients:

- [ ] 1/4 cup plus 2 tablespoons coconut oil, melted
- [ ] 1/4 cup plus 2 tablespoons warm water
- [ ] 3 cups coconut flakes, unsweetened
- [ ] 3 eggs, beaten
- [ ] Stevia, to taste (about 3 droppers full or equivalent low carb sweetener)

If making chocolate macaroons:

☐ 1/3 cups raw cacao powder, optional
☐ Almond, vanilla, or other extract you prefer

Directions:

1. Preheat oven to 400F.
2. In a large bowl, combine the coconut oil, coconut flakes, and warm water.
3. Stir thoroughly until the coconut flakes are saturated with the oil and water.
4. In a small mixing bowl, combine the stevia and the eggs thoroughly.
5. Pour the egg mixture into the coconut flake mixture. Stir well.
6. If you want to make chocolate macaroons, divide the mixture into two equal amounts. Mix 1/2 of the mixture with cocoa powder and your preferred extract. Add more stevia if you prefer to sweeten the chocolate mixture since cacao is bitter.
7. with a small scoop, scoop out an amount of the mixture and place into an ungreased cookie sheet or baking stone.
8. Bake for about 12-15 minutes.
9. Allow the macaroons to cool before removing from the pan.
10. Store in gallon freezer bags and keep in the fridge or freezer.

Peanut Butter Balls

These completely sugar-free, low carb balls are creamy with the delicious sweet taste of peanut butter. They are very simple to make, but are absolutely scrumptious!

Serves: 12
Prep time: 40 minutes
Cook time: 0 minutes

Nutritional Facts
Serving Size: 10 g

Calories: 58
Total Fat: 5.7 g
Saturated Fat: 2.2 g   **Trans Fat:** 0 g
Cholesterol: 9 mg
Sodium: 27 mg
Potassium: 40 mg
Total Carbohydrates: 1.2 g
Dietary Fibre: 0.0 g   **Sugars:** 0.0 g
Protein: 1.3 g
Vitamin A: 2%   **Vitamin C:** 0 %
Calcium: 1%   **Iron:** 2%

Ingredients:
- ☐ 2 tablespoons peanut butter, homemade
- ☐ 2 tablespoons almond butter, homemade
- ☐ 2 tablespoons butter, grass-fed
- ☐ 2 tablespoons heavy cream
- ☐ 1 1/2 teaspoon erythritol
- ☐ 4 drops liquid stevia

Directions:
1. In a bowl add all ingredients and mix well until even.
2. Freeze for 40 minutes.
3. Now make small round balls and transfer into serving dish.
4. Serve and enjoy.

Fudge Brownie

Fudge brownies are always a hit with the kids! This dessert is loaded with healthy fats and is also nut-free.

Serves: 16
Prep. Time: 20 minutes
Cook Time: 20-25 minutes

Nutritional Facts
Serving Size: 51 g

Calories: 165
Total Fat: 15.5 g
Saturated Fat: 13.2 g   **Trans Fat:** 0.0 g
Cholesterol: 14 mg
Sodium: 73 mg
Potassium: 193 mg
Total Carbohydrates: 9.2 g
Dietary Fibre: 5.1 g   **Sugars:** 2.6 g
Protein: 2.1 g
Vitamin A: 1 %   **Vitamin C:** 4 %,
Calcium: 1 %   **Iron:** 31 %

Ingredients:
- [ ] 5 tablespoons cacao powder
- [ ] 3/4-1 cup granulated sweetener
- [ ] 3/4 cup coconut butter, melted
- [ ] 2 teaspoons vanilla extract
- [ ] 2 tablespoon butter, grass-fed, melted (ghee or coconut oil will work as well)
- [ ] 1/4 teaspoon sea salt
- [ ] 1/4 teaspoon baking soda

- ☐ 1/3 cup coconut milk cream, full-fat (the cream on a chilled can of coconut milk)
- ☐ 1 egg

Optional:
- ☐ 1/2 teaspoon vanilla bean powder

Directions:
1. In a bowl, combine the cocoa powder, (if using) vanilla bean powder, sweetener, salt, baking soda. Set aside.
2. Put the coconut butter, butter, and coconut cream in another bowl. Beat until the mixture is smooth.
3. Add the egg and the vanilla extract. Beat until well combined.
4. Add the cocoa powder mix into the coconut butter mix. Beat until the lumps are gone.
5. Depending on how thick you want your truffles, spread the mixture into a 6x6-inch or 8x8-inch greased pan.
6. Bake at 350F for about 20-25 minutes, or until the edges are brown. If you bake the mixture in a 6x6-inch pan, the centre will look uncooked, but it will be okay.
7. Let the pan cool. When the pan is cooled, put in the refrigerator. Cool completely.
8. Keep stored in the fridge.

Pumpkin Pie Collagen Patties

The added collagen has many added health benefits including keeping you feel full longer, aid in weight loss and stimulates growth hormones. Collagen hydrolysate virtually has no taste and does not coagulate so you can add it to anything, even to smoothies and beverages. If you are vegan, then you can opt not to add collagen and the recipe will still taste the same.

Serves: 18
Prep. Time: 20 minutes
Cook Time: 60 minutes

Nutritional Facts
Serving Size: 30 g

Calories: 102
Total Fat: 9.8 g
Saturated Fat: 8.5 g   **Trans Fat:** 0.0 g
Cholesterol: 0 mg
Sodium: 33 mg
Potassium: 65 mg
Total Carbohydrates: 3.1 g
Dietary Fibre: 1.6 g   **Sugars:** 1.1 g
Protein: 1.9 g
Vitamin A: 32 %   **Vitamin C:** 2 %,
Calcium: 1 %   **Iron:** 10 %

Ingredients:
- ☐ 7 ounces long-shredded coconut, unsweetened
- ☐ 3/4 cup pumpkin puree, unsweetened
- ☐ 25 drops stevia extract, alcohol-free
- ☐ 1/4 teaspoon vanilla extract, pure, alcohol-free

- ☐ 1/4 cup collagen, optional
- ☐ 1/2 cup coconut oil
- ☐ 1 tablespoon ground cinnamon
- ☐ 1 1/2 teaspoons ginger, ground
- ☐ Pinch ground cloves
- ☐ Pinch to 1/4 teaspoon Himalayan rock salt

Directions:

1. Line a baking sheet with 2 pieces 12-mold mini muffin silicon molds. Set aside.
2. Put the coconut oil, shredded coconut, salt and stevia in the bowl of a food processor.
3. Process for about 5-8 minutes on high until the mixture is drippy. Remove the lid and scrape the chunky bits from the side of the bowl when needed.
4. When smooth, reserve 1/4 cup of the mixture, leaving the remaining in the bowl.
5. Add the remaining ingredients into the bowl. Continue processing until the mixture is smooth again. If you are using cold pumpkin puree, the coconut will harden. If this happens, just process until the mixture is smooth again. The texture of the mixture will be similar to applesauce.
6. Scoop about 2 teaspoons of the pumpkin mixture into each muffin cup. Press down with the back of the spoon or with your fingers to flatten completely.
7. Top with the reserved coconut mixture.
8. Transfer the baking sheet into the freezer. Freeze for about 1 hour or until solid.

Bacon and Pecan Chocolate Bark

Who doesn't love bacon? Who doesn't love chocolate? If someone asked me which one I love more, I wouldn't be able to choose! The salty bacon and sweet chocolate taste combine to make an absolutely delightful treat!

Serves: 20
Prep. Time: 30 minutes, plus 1 hour and more freezing time
Cook Time: 30 minutes

Nutritional Facts
Serving Size: 45 g

Calories: 246
Total Fat: 22.9 g
Saturated Fat: 4.8 g   **Trans Fat:** 0.0 g
Cholesterol: 14 mg
Sodium: 299 mg
Potassium: 288 mg
Total Carbohydrates: 8.8 g
Dietary Fibre: 4.8 g   **Sugars:** 0.7 g
Protein: 8.3 g
Vitamin A: 1 %   **Vitamin C:** 0 %,
Calcium: 4 %   **Iron:** 11 %

Ingredients:
For the bacon-pecan crumble:
- ☐ 2 tablespoons water
- ☐ 1/2 cup <u>Swerve</u> Sweetener or any low carb sweetener equivalent
- ☐ 1 tablespoon butter
- ☐ 1/2 pound bacon, chopped, cooked until crisp

- [ ] 1 1/2 cups pecans, toasted, chopped

For the chocolate mixture:
- [ ] 4 ounces cocoa butter
- [ ] 3/4 cup cocoa powder
- [ ] 2 1/2 ounces unsweetened chocolate
- [ ] 1/4 teaspoon kosher salt
- [ ] 1/2 teaspoon vanilla extract
- [ ] 1/2 cup powdered Swerve Sweetener, sifted

Directions:
1. Line a baking sheet with parchment paper.
2. Line a 9x13-inch pan with another parchment paper.
3. In a medium saucepan over medium heat, combine the water and the 1/2 cup Swerve Sweetener, stirring occasionally. Bring the mixture to a boil and cook for about 7-9 minutes or until the mixture darkens. The mixture will smoke slightly. This will be normal.
4. Remove the saucepan from the heat.
5. Whisk the butter in. Add the bacon and the pecans. Quickly stir to coat and then stir in the salt.
6. Spread the bacon-pecan mixture into the prepared baking sheet. Allow to cool and then break up into clumps.
7. In a heavy saucepan, melt the chocolate and the butter together until the mixture is smooth.
8. Stir in the powdered sweetener and cocoa powder until the mixture is smooth.
9. Remove from the heat. Stir in the vanilla extract.
10. Stir the crumbled bacon-pecan mixture into the chocolate mixture.

11. Spread the mixture into the prepared 9x13-inch pan.
12. Refrigerate for at least 1 hour or until the mixture is solid.
13. When solid, cut into barks.

Molding Tip:
Alternatively, you can make clusters. Spoon mixture into mini muffin ciups lined with foil or parchment mini-cupcake liners.

You can also spoon the mixture into various candy molds.

Coffee Chocolate Coconut Truffle

This dessert can be eaten straight from the bowl. I definitely do this when I'm feeling lazy. You can also pack the mixture in to ice cube moulds. They are handy to enjoy later on as a snack with a cup of coffee or tea.

Serves: 6
Prep. Time: 10 mins, plus 4-5 hours freezing
Cook Time: 0 minutes

Nutritional Facts
Serving Size: 23 g

Calories: 90
Total Fat: 9.2 g
Saturated Fat: 7.5 g   **Trans Fat:** 0.0 g
Cholesterol: 0 mg
Sodium: 4 mg
Potassium: 86 mg
Total Carbohydrates: 3.7 g
Dietary Fibre: 2.1 g   **Sugars:** 0.9 g
Protein: 1.0 g
Vitamin A: 0 %   **Vitamin C:** 1 %,
Calcium: 4 %   **Iron:** 15 %

Ingredients:
- [ ] 3 tablespoons cocoa powder (100%)
- [ ] 1/2 teaspoon raw honey (or equivalent low carb sweetener)
- [ ] 1/2 cup coconut butter, melted
- [ ] 1 tablespoon unsweetened coconut flakes
- [ ] 1 tablespoon ground coffee
- [ ] 1 tablespoon coconut oil

Directions:
1. Melt the coconut butter in a microwave so that it can be mixed using fork.
2. Mix all of the remaining in a bowl using a fork.
3. Spoon the mixture into 6 ice cube molds. Gently pat the mixture into the molds with the fork.
4. Freeze for about 4-5 hours.
5. To serve, defrost at temperature for about 15-20 minutes. Enjoy!

Whipped Coconut Cream with Berries

This dairy fee recipe is a delicious way to consume healthy fat into your diet. It's simple to make and you can flavour it with your choice of berries with some chocolate chips.

Serves: 2
Prep. Time: 5 minutes, plus 12-24 hours freezing
Cook Time: 0 minutes

Nutritional Facts

Serving Size: 261 g

Calories: 480
Total Fat: 45.9 g
Saturated Fat: 40.5 g   **Trans Fat:** 0.0 g
Cholesterol: 0 mg
Sodium: 29 mg
Potassium: 593 mg
Total Carbohydrates: 19.1 g
Dietary Fibre: 6.7 g   **Sugars:** 11.4 g
Protein: 4.9 g
Vitamin A: 0 %   **Vitamin C:** 34 %,
Calcium: 4 %   **Iron:** 19 %

Ingredients:
- ☐ 1 can coconut milk, unsweetened, full-fat
- ☐ Berries of choice

Optional:
- ☐ Dark chocolate

☐ Dash of vanilla

Directions:
1. Refrigerate the coconut milk for at least 12 hours to overnight.
2. Scoop out the coconut cream, leaving the water.
3. Whip the coconut cream with a hand mixer for about 2-3 mixer.
4. Add the berries (blueberries and strawberries are perfect for this).
5. Top with chocolate shavings and dash of vanilla, if desired.

Note:
Reserve the coconut water and use in your low carb smoothies.

Coconut Cream Chocolate Mousse

One of the easiest low carb desserts that you can enjoy is this mouse. Enjoy these treats topped with your favourite fruits. For added crunch, top with shredded dark chocolate.

Serves: 1
Prep. Time: 10 minutes, plus 12-24 hours chilling
Cook Time: 0 minutes

Nutritional Facts
Serving Size: 105 g

Calories: 246
Total Fat: 24.6 g
Saturated Fat: 21.3 g   **Trans Fat:** 0.0 g
Cholesterol: 0 mg
Sodium: 16 mg
Potassium: 345 mg
Total Carbohydrates: 9.4 g
Dietary Fibre: 4.1 g   **Sugars:** 3.5 g
Protein: 3.0 g
Vitamin A: 0 %   **Vitamin C:** 4 %,
Calcium: 2 %   **Iron:** 14 %

Ingredients:
- [ ] 4 teaspoons chocolate chips, unsweetened
- [ ] 2 teaspoons vanilla extract
- [ ] 2 tablespoons glycemic sweetener
- [ ] 2 tablespoons cocoa powder, sifted
- [ ] 1 can coconut milk, full fat, chilled for 12-24 hours

Directions:
1. Refrigerate the coconut milk can, when chilled, open and scoop out the cream. Reserve the coconut water for other uses.
2. Put the coconut cream into the bowl of a stand mixer.
3. Add the sweetener, vanilla extract and cocoa powder. Whip it up.

Chapter 9: Smoothies

Peanut Butter Caramel Shake

This frosty coconut milk shake is flavoured with peanut butter and jazzed with salted caramel is absolutely delectable. This frozen treat is a good source of iron and fibre.

Serves: 2
Prep time: 5 minutes
Cook time: 0 minutes

Nutritional Facts
Serving Size: 271 g

Calories: 472
Total Fat: 48.2 g
Saturated Fat: 34.4 g   **Trans Fat:** 0.0 g
Cholesterol: 31 mg
Sodium: 201 mg
Potassium: 424 mg
Total Carbohydrates: 12 g
Dietary Fibre: 5.0 g   **Sugars:** 5.5 g
Protein: 6.9 g
Vitamin A: 7 %   **Vitamin C:** 6 %,
Calcium: 3 %   **Iron:** 19 %

Ingredients:
- [ ] 7 Ice cubes
- [ ] 1 cup coconut Milk
- [ ] 2 tablespoons peanut butter
- [ ] 1 tablespoon maple syrup
- [ ] 2 tablespoon of Torani salted caramel

☐   1/4 tsp. xanthan gum

Directions:
1. In a blender add all ingredients and blend until smooth and creamy.
2. Pour into glass and serve.

Cocoa-Coconut- Macadamia Smoothie

This tasty smoothie is a drink, dessert, snack, and fat bomb all rolled into one. This dairy-free treat is packed with healthy good fats, which help you feel full longer.

Serves: 2
Prep. Time: 5 minutes
Cook Time: 0 minutes

Nutritional Facts

Serving Size: 224 g

Calories: 279
Total Fat: 28.2 g
Saturated Fat: 20.3 g   **Trans Fat:** 0.0 g
Cholesterol: 0 mg
Sodium: 96 mg
Potassium: 313 mg
Total Carbohydrates: 10.9 g
Dietary Fibre: 5.1 g   **Sugars:** 3.7 g
Protein: 3.2 g
Vitamin A: 0 %   **Vitamin C:** 4 %,
Calcium: 3 %   **Iron:** 12 %

Ingredients:

- ☐ 1 cup ice cubes
- ☐ 1 dash salt
- ☐ 1 tablespoon cocoa powder, unsweetened
- ☐ 1/2 teaspoon vanilla extract
- ☐ 2 tablespoons macadamia nuts, crushed salted

- ☐ 2 tablespoons Swerve or other low carb sugar equivalent
- ☐ 3/4 cup coconut milk, unsweetened

Directions:
1. Put all of the ingredients in a blender.
2. Blend until yummy smooth.
3. Pour into two glasses.
4. Top each serve with whipped coconut cream, macadamia nuts, and toasted coconuts.

Spinach Avocado Banana Smoothie

This quick to make a delicious smoothie can be enjoyed as a breakfast or snack drink. With only a few ingredients, this smoothie is packed with nutrients that will give you the boost you need in the morning.

Serves: 5
Prep. Time: 3 minutes
Blend Time: 2 minutes

Nutritional Facts
Serving Size: 296 g
Calories: 197
Total Fat: 8 g
Saturated Fat: 1.7 g   **Trans. Fat:** 0 g
Cholesterol: 0 mg
Sodium: 62 mg
Potassium: 367 mg
Total Carbohydrates: 13.6 g
Dietary Fiber: 3.7 g   **Sugar:** 7 g
Protein: 20.6 g
Vitamin A: 24%   **Vitamin C:** 16%
Calcium: 4%   **Iron:** 5%

Ingredients:
- 2 cups spinach
- 1 large banana, frozen
- 1 avocado
- 1 tablespoon honey
- 1 pack gelatin or 1 scoop isolate protein

- 1 cup water
- 3 cups ice

Directions :
1. Put all of the ingredients into the blender. Blend
   until smooth.

Almond Avocado Smoothie

The key to this smoothie is choosing a good almond butter. You will get most of your flavor from the almond butter you pick. Almond butter contains copper and calcium, both of which play a vital role in maintaining a healthy nervous system and healthy brain cells. Almond butter is also rich in vitamin E, magnesium, fiber, and healthy unsaturated fatty acids.

Serves: 2
Prep. Time: 3 minutes
Blend Time: 2 minutes

Nutritional Facts
Serving Size: 214 g
Calories: 359
Total Fat: 22.2 g
Saturated Fat: 6.9 g   **Trans. Fat:** 0 g
Cholesterol: 22 mg
Sodium: 128 mg
Potassium: 437 mg
Total Carbohydrates: 13.1 g
Dietary Fiber: 4 g   **Sugar:** 4.5 g
Protein: 28.7 g
Vitamin A: 6%   **Vitamin C:** 9%
Calcium: 18%   **Iron:** 6%

Ingredients:
- 1/2 avocado, peeled, pitted, sliced
- 1/2 cup half and half
- 1/2 cup unsweetened almond milk, vanilla
- 1/2 teaspoon vanilla extract
- 2 scoops vanilla isolate protein

- 1 tablespoon almond butter
- Pinch of cinnamon
- 1 packet stevia
- 2-4 ice cubes

Directions :

2. Put everything in a blender except the ice cubes. Blend for until smooth.
3. Add in ice cubes. Blend again.
4. Pour in a glass. Enjoy!

Almond Strawberry Delight

This refreshing smoothie is nutty with a creamy sweet taste. Aside from antioxidants, strawberries also potassium, folate, dietary fiber, manganese. Some of the health benefits include eye improvement and relief from arthritis, gout, high blood pressure, and various other cardiovascular related diseases.

Serves: 2
Prep. Time: 3 minutes
Blend Time: 2 minutes

Nutritional Facts
Serving Size: 334 g

Calories: 352
Total Fat: 24.2 g
Saturated Fat: 13.3 g   **Trans. Fat:** 0 g
Cholesterol: 78 mg
Sodium: 240 mg
Potassium: 219 mg
Total Carbohydrates: 9 g
Dietary Fiber: 1.3 g   **Sugar:** 5.2 g
Protein: 26 g
Vitamin A: 17%   **Vitamin C:** 12%
Calcium: 33% **Iron:** 6%

Ingredients:
- 16 ounces unsweetened almond milk, vanilla
- 1 packet stevia
- 4-ounce heavy cream
- 2 scoops vanilla isolate protein or 4 tablespoons gelatin plus 1 teaspoon vanilla extract
- 1/4 cup frozen strawberries, unsweetened

Directions :
1. Put everything in a blender. Blend for until smooth.
   Pour in a glass. Enjoy!

Creamy Blackberry

This drink delicious smoothie is packed with anthocyanins, which are compounds that help keep the heart healthy. The fiber and magnesium of blackberries also promotes strong blood flow and prevents blockage in the arteries, which reduces the risk of strokes and heart attacks..

Serves: 2
Prep. Time: 3 minutes
Blend Time: 2 minutes

Nutritional Facts
Serving Size: 268 g

Calories: 300
Total Fat: 17 g
Saturated Fat: 10.4 g   **Trans. Fat:** 0 g
Cholesterol: 62 mg
Sodium: 76 mg
Potassium: 156 mg
Total Carbohydrates: 12.2 g
Dietary Fiber: 3.8 g   **Sugar:** 7.6 g
Protein: 25.9 g
Vitamin A: 16%   **Vitamin C:** 26%
Calcium: 7%   **Iron:** 4%

Ingredients:
- 1 cup fresh blackberries
- 1 packet stevia
- 3/4 cup heavy whipping cream
- 2 scoops vanilla isolate protein or 4 tablespoons gelatin plus 2 teaspoon vanilla extract
- 1 cup ice cubes

Directions :
1. Put everything in a blender except the ice cubes. Blend for until smooth.
2. Add in ice cubes. Blend again.
3. Pour in a glass. Enjoy!

Creamy Chocolate Milkshake

This is a quick and easy way to make your own keto friendly chocolate milkshake. This low carb version is delicious but because you can eat a lot of fat you can enjoy it guilt free!

Serves: 2
Prep. Time: 3 minutes
Blend Time: 2 minutes

Nutritional Facts
Serving Size: 361 g

Calories: 120
Total Fat: 24.2 g
Saturated Fat: 13.3 g   **Trans. Fat:** 0 g
Cholesterol: 78 mg
Sodium: 214 mg
Potassium: 218 mg
Total Carbohydrates: 7.4 g
Dietary Fiber: 0.9 g   **Sugar:** 4.1 g
Protein: 14.1 g
Vitamin A: 17%   **Vitamin C:** 1%
Calcium: 32% **Iron:** 5%

Ingredients:
- 16 ounces unsweetened almond milk, vanilla
- 4 ounces heavy cream
- 1 scoop chocolate isolate protein
- 1 packet stevia

• 1/2 cup crushed ice

Directions :
1. Put everything in a blender except the ice cubes.
   Blend for until smooth.
2. Add in the ice cubes. Blend again.
3. Pour in a glass. Enjoy!

***

Hazelnut Keto Coffee Smoothie

This smoothie combines hazelnut flavor and coffee into a delicious dessert that will start your day off with a tasty bang!

Serves: 1
Prep. Time: 3 minutes
Blend Time: 2 minutes

Nutritional Facts

Serving Size: 286 g

Calories: 19
Total Fat: 20.6 g
Saturated Fat: 9.6 g   **Trans. Fat:** 0 g
Cholesterol: 55 mg
Sodium: 20 mg
Potassium: 210 mg
Total Carbohydrates: 2.7 g
Dietary Fiber: 0.9 g   **Sugar:** 0 g
Protein: 2.5 g
Vitamin A: 12%   **Vitamin C:** 1%
Calcium: 4%   **Iron:** 3%

Ingredients:

- 1/3 cup heavy cream
- 1 cup cold coffee
- 1-2 tablespoon hazelnut syrup, sugar-free
- Ice cubes

Directions :
1. Put everything in a blender except the ice cubes.
   Blend for until smooth.
2. Add in ice cubes. Blend again.
3. Pour in a glass. Enjoy!

The Peanut Milkshake

Peanut butter is not just for your kid's lunch! This versatile spread is high in healthy oils and protein, which help aid weight loss, diabetes, and Alzheimer's disease. Peanuts also contain fiber for a healthy bowel movement, magnesium for muscle and bone health.

Serves: 2
Prep. Time: 3 minutes
Blend Time: 2 minutes

Nutritional Facts
Serving Size: 326g

Calories: 278
Total Fat: 24.1 g
Saturated Fat: 14.5 g   **Trans. Fat:** 0 g
Cholesterol: 0 mg
Sodium: 176 mg
Potassium: 361 mg
Total Carbohydrates: 11.7g
Dietary Fiber: 2.8 g   **Sugar:** 7.8 g
Protein: 5.9 g
Vitamin A: 0%   **Vitamin C:** 3%
Calcium: 16% **Iron:** 16%

Ingredients:
- 2 tablespoons peanut butter, all-natural
- 1 tsp vanilla extract
- 1 packet stevia
- 1 cup unsweetened almond milk, vanilla
- 1/2 cup coconut milk, regular

- 1 cup ice cubes

Directions :
1. Put everything in a blender except the ice cubes. Blend for until smooth.
2. Add in ice cubes. Blend again.
3. Pour in a glass. Enjoy!

The Keto Frapp

This dairy-free, sugar-free, completely keto and vegan-friendly smoothie is a great way to kick off your fat-burning morning. This simple and tasty drink sneaks added nutrients in with grounded flax seeds.

Serves: 1
Prep. Time: 3 minutes
Blend Time: 2 minutes

Nutritional Facts

Serving Size: 295 g

Calories: 226
Total Fat: 19.5 g
Saturated Fat: 9.8 g   **Trans. Fat:** 0 g
Cholesterol: 55 mg
Sodium: 24 mg
Potassium: 266 mg
Total Carbohydrates: 5.7 g
Fiber: 3.8 g   **Sugar:** 0.8 g
Protein: 3.7 g
Vitamin A: 12%   **Vitamin C:** 0%
Calcium: 4%   **Iron:** 22%

Ingredients:
- 1 cup leftover or cold coffee

- 1 teaspoon vanilla extract
- 1/3 cup heavy cream
- 1-2 tablespoons ground flax seeds
- 6 ice cubes

Optional: for a sweeter blend
- 2 tablespoons salted caramel syrup, sugar-free

Directions :
1. Put everything in a blender except the ice cubes. Blend for until smooth.
2. Add in ice cubes. Blend again.
3. Pour in a glass.
4. Add caramel syrup, if desired. Enjoy!

Apricot, Peach, and Coconut Smoothie

Apricots blend well with coconut and other tropical fruits. Blending them with peaches and coconut milk is a yummy alternative.

Serves: 4
Prep. Time: 3 minutes
Blend Time: 2 minutes

Nutritional Facts
Serving Size: 230g

Calories: 236
Total Fat: 10.6 g
Saturated Fat: 9 g **Trans. Fat:** 0 g
Cholesterol: 0 mg
Sodium: 64 mg
Potassium: 348 mg
Total Carbohydrates: 12.8 g
Dietary Fiber: 2.7 g   **Sugar:** 10.2 g
Protein: 26.1 g
Vitamin A: 25%   **Vitamin C:** 16%
Calcium: 3%   **Iron:** 7%

Ingredients:
- 6 ounces coconut milk
- 1 cup peaches
- 1 1/2 cup apricot

- 4 pack gelatin
- 1 cup ice cubes

Directions :

1. Put all of the ingredients into the blender. Blend until smooth.

Creamy Blackberry Smoothie

Blackberries make this smoothie rich in Vitamin C and bioflavonoids. These berries have one of the highest antioxidant levels of all fruits, which give them their dark blue color. Bioflavonoids help make the skin look younger, keeps the brain alert, and helps maintain your memory. Blueberries are also high in tannin, which helps you 'down there' by helping to alleviate hemorrhoids, reduce inflammation in the intestine, and soothe diarrhea.

Serves: 2
Prep. Time: 3 minutes
Blend Time: 2 minutes

Nutritional Facts
Serving Size: 268 g

Calories: 300
Total Fat 17 g
Saturated Fat: 10.4 g   **Trans. Fat:** 0 g
Cholesterol: 62 mg
Sodium: 76 mg
Potassium: 156 mg
Total Carbohydrates: 12.2 g
Dietary Fiber: 3.8 g   **Sugar:** 7.6 g
Protein: 25.9 g
Vitamin A: 16%   **Vitamin C:** 26%
Calcium: 7%   **Iron:** 4%

Ingredients:
- 1 cup fresh blackberries
- 1 packet stevia
- 3/4 cup heavy whipping cream
- 2 scoops vanilla isolate protein or 4 tablespoons gelatin plus 2 teaspoon vanilla extract
- 1 cup ice cubes

Directions :
4. Put everything in a blender except the ice cubes. Blend for until smooth.
5. Add in ice cubes. Blend again.
6. Pour in a glass. Enjoy!

Cinnamon Bun Smoothie

This delicious smoothie contains Chia seeds, which are packed with nutrients. In fact, chia is an ancient Mayan word for "strength". These seeds are loaded with protein, fiber, omega 3 fatty acids, and other micronutrients. They are also rich in calcium, magnesium, manganese, and phosphorus.

Serves: 1
Prep. Time: 3 minutes
Blend Time: 2 minutes

Nutritional Facts
Serving Size: 532 g

Calories: 217
Total Fat: 24.2 g
Saturated Fat: 0.6 g   **Trans. Fat:** 0 g
Cholesterol: 0 mg
Sodium: 244 mg
Potassium: 260 mg
Total Carbohydrates: 13.1 g
Dietary Fiber: 3.5 g   **Sugar:** 8.2 g
Protein: 26.3 g
Vitamin A: 0%   **Vitamin C:** 0%
Calcium: 34%   **Iron:** 17%

Ingredients:
- 1/4 tsp vanilla extract
- 1/2 tsp cinnamon

- 1 cup unsweetened almond milk
- 1 packet stevia
- 1 tbsp. chia seeds or flax seeds
- 2 tbsp. vanilla protein powder or 2 tablespoons gelatin plus 1 teaspoon vanilla extract
- 1 cup ice cubes

Directions :

1. Put everything in a blender except the ice cubes. Blend for until smooth.
2. Add in the ice cubes. Blend again.
3. Pour in a glass. Enjoy!

Super Strawberry Cheesecake Smoothie

This simple creamy thick smoothie is sweet and has an indulgent strawberry cheesecake flavor that will satisfy your taste buds. The secret of this drink is the goodness of cream cheese, which gives it that creamy tang taste that we all love.

Serves: 2
Prep. Time: 3 minutes
Blend Time: 2 minutes

Nutritional Facts
Serving Size: 138 g

Calories: 164
Total Fat: 10.8 g
Saturated Fat: 6.3 g   **Trans. Fat:** 0 g
Cholesterol: 31 mg
Sodium: 129 mg
Potassium: 83 mg
Total Carbohydrates: 12.6 g
Dietary Fiber: 1 g **Sugar:** 10.4 g
Protein: 2.4 g
Vitamin A: 8%   **Vitamin C:** 23%
Calcium: 10% **Iron:** 4%

Ingredients:

- 1/2 cup frozen strawberries, unsweetened
- 1/2 cup unsweetened almond milk, vanilla
- 1/2 teaspoons vanilla extract
- 2 ounces cream cheese, regular
- 2 packets stevia or 4 teaspoons Splenda
- 3-4 ice cubes

Directions :
1. Put everything in a blender except the ice cubes. Blend for until smooth.
2. Add in ice cubes. Blend again.
3. Pour in a glass. Enjoy!

Raspberry Cheesecake Smoothie

Like the Super Strawberry-Cheesecake Smoothie, this version is a yummy smoothie with a creamy, sweet cheesecake flavor. The cottage cheese adds protein to the blend and keeps the carbs low. The protein content of this cheese is casein, which make you feel full longer and helps build muscle.

Serves: 1
Prep. Time: 3 minutes
Blend Time: 2 minutes

Nutritional Facts

Serving Size: 353 g

Calories: 208
Total Fat: 13.8 g
Saturated Fat: 6.5 g   **Trans. Fat:** 0 g
Cholesterol: 31 mg
Sodium: 266 mg
Potassium: 336 mg
Total Carbohydrates: 11.7 g
Dietary Fiber: 5.0 g   **Sugar:** 4.4 g
Protein: 3.9 g
Vitamin A: 8%   **Vitamin C:** 27%
Calcium: 34%   **Iron:** 8%

Ingredients:
- 1 cup unsweetened almond milk

- 1/2 cup raspberries
- 1 ounce cream cheese
- 1 tablespoon vanilla syrup, sugar-free
- 4 Ice cubes

Directions :
1. Put everything in a blender except the ice cubes.
   Blend for until smooth.
2. Add in ice cubes. Blend again.
3. Pour in a glass. Enjoy!

Cinnamon Strawberry-Almond Smoothie

Adding almond nuts to a strawberry smoothie gives it a delicious crunchy texture. It also packs the smoothie the nutrients L-carnitine (known for its weight loss properties) and riboflavin, which help boost brain activity and reduce the risk of Alzheimer's disease.

Serves: 1
Prep. Time: 3 minutes
Blend Time: 2 minutes

Nutritional Facts
Serving Size: 335 g

Calories: 135
Total Fat: 9.7 g
Saturated Fat: 0.8 g   **Trans. Fat:** 0 g
Cholesterol: 0 mg
Sodium: 181 mg
Potassium: 392 mg
Total Carbohydrates: 11 g
Dietary Fiber: 4.5 g   **Sugar:** 4 g
Protein: 4 g
Vitamin A: 0%   **Vitamin C:** 71%
Calcium: 36%   **Iron:** 9%

Ingredients:
- 2 tablespoons almonds
- 1/2 teaspoon cinnamon
- 1/2 cup organic strawberries, frozen
- 1 cup unsweetened almond milk, vanilla
- 2 iced cubes

Optional:
- 1 tablespoon chia seeds or flax seeds

Directions :
1. Put everything in a blender. Blend for until smooth. Pour in a glass., add iced cubes and enjoy!

Buttered Coffee Pumpkin Pie

While most of the pumpkin-flavored treats should be enjoyed occasionally, you can sip on this low carb smoothie every day. Plus this guilt-free smoothie is packed with 102% of your daily intake of vitamin A.

Serves: 1
Prep. Time: 3 minutes
Blend Time: 2 minutes

Nutritional Facts

Serving Size: 393 g

Calories: 157
Total Fat: 11.7 g
Saturated Fat: 7.4 g   **Trans. Fat:** 0 g
Cholesterol: 31 mg
Sodium: 90 mg
Potassium: 236 mg
Total Carbohydrates: 10.8 g
Dietary Fiber: 0.9 g   **Sugar:** 9.1 g
Protein: 0.9 g
Vitamin A: 102%   **Vitamin C:** 2%
Calcium: 2%   **Iron:** 3%

Ingredients:

- 1/4 teaspoon pumpkin pie spice
- 1 tablespoon regular butter, unsalted
- 12 ounces hot coffee
- 2 tablespoons canned pumpkin

- 1 packet stevia

Directions:
1. Put everything in a blender. Blend for until smooth. Pour in a glass. Enjoy!

Vanilla Chocolate Spice Shake

This smoothie is a unique treat. This cold blend is spiked with the surprising touch of cayenne heat. Cayenne is a spice known to neutralize acidity and stimulate circulation. This makes it a well-known ingredient in detoxifying and cleansing regimes.

Serves: 2
Prep. Time: 3 minutes
Blend Time: 2 minutes

Nutritional Facts
Serving Size: 171 g

Calories: 218
Total Fat: 22.6 g
Saturated Fat: 18.7 g   **Trans. Fat:** 0 g
Cholesterol: 0 mg
Sodium: 10 mg
Potassium: 246 mg
Total Carbohydrates: 5.8 g
Dietary Fiber: 3.3 g   **Sugar:** 1.2 g
Protein: 2.3 g
Vitamin A: 1%   **Vitamin C:** 2%
Calcium: 2%   **Iron:** 13%

Ingredients:
- 1/4 cup coconut cream

- 1/2 - 1 cup water
- 1/2 pinch cayenne powder
- 1 tbsp. flax seeds or chia seeds
- 2 tbsp. unsweetened cocoa powder
- 2 tbsp. unrefined coconut oil
- Dash of vanilla extract
- Pinch of ground cinnamon
- Ice cubes, if desired

Directions :

1.   Put everything in a blender except the ice cubes. Blend for until smooth.
2.   Add in the ice cubes. Blend again.
3.   Pour in a glass. Enjoy!

Heavenly Creamy Chocolate Shake

Whipping cream makes this shake light as air and creamy. This out of this world sensational drink is also high is calcium.

Serves: 1
Prep. Time: 3 minutes
Blend Time: 2 minutes

Nutritional Facts

Serving Size: 306 g

Calories: 236
Total Fat: 19 g
Saturated Fat: 10 g   **Trans. Fat:** 0 g
Cholesterol: 55 mg
Sodium: 197 mg
Potassium: 305 mg
Total Carbohydrates: 14.3 g
Dietary Fiber: 2.8 g   **Sugar:** 8.4g
Protein: 2.9 g
Vitamin A: 12%   **Vitamin C:** 0%
Calcium: 33%   **Iron:** 8%

Ingredients:

- 1 cup unsweetened almond milk
- 1/3 cup heavy whipping cream
- 1 packet stevia
- 1/2 teaspoon vanilla extract

- 1 tablespoon unsweetened cocoa powder
- 3 ice cubes

Directions :

1. Put everything in a blender except the ice cubes. Blend for until smooth.
2. Add in ice cubes. Blend again.
3. Pour in a glass. Enjoy!

Creamy Avocado Chocolate Smoothie

The avocado in this smoothie makes for a sinfully delicious drink. Rich, creamy, and velvety smooth. The avocado also packs this drink with a healthy amount of good fats.

Serves: 2
Prep. Time: 3 minutes
Blend Time: 2 minutes

Nutritional Facts
Serving Size: 286 g

Calories: 450
Total Fat: 32.3 g
Saturated Fat: 12.1 g   **Trans. Fat:** 0 g
Cholesterol: 42 mg
Sodium: 53 mg
Potassium: 535 mg
Total Carbohydrates: 16.6 g
Dietary Fiber: 6.9 g   **Sugar:** 7.2 g
Protein: 26.9 g
Vitamin A: 12%   **Vitamin C:** 17%
Calcium: 6%   **Iron:** 6%

Ingredients:
- 1 avocado, frozen
- 1/2 cup heavy cream
- 1 tablespoon dark chocolate

- 1 teaspoon Splenda
- 1 pack gelatin or 1 scoop chocolate isolate protein
- 1 cup water

Directions :
1. Put all of the ingredients into the blender. Blend until smooth

Peach Coconut Smoothie

Fresh summer peaches and coconut milk make this a sweet, creamy dairy-free blend. Using chilled coconut milk gives it a milkshake-like consistency. The coconut milk also makes it extra rich and creamy with the high amount of healthy fats.

Serves: 2
Prep. Time: 3 minutes
Blend Time: 2 minutes

Nutritional Facts
Serving Size: 342 g

Calories: 399
Total Fat: 28.8 g
Saturated Fat: 25.4 g   **Trans. Fat:** 0 g
Cholesterol: 0 mg
Sodium: 76 mg
Potassium: 464 mg
Total Carbohydrates: 13.9 g
Dietary Fiber: 3.8 g   **Sugar:** 10.2 g
Protein: 27.4 g
Vitamin A: 5%   **Vitamin C:** 16%
Calcium: 4%   **Iron:** 14%

Ingredients:
- 1 1/2 peaches, frozen
- 1 cup coconut milk
- 1 tsp. lemon zest
- 2 pack gelatin

- 1 cup ice

Directions :
1. Put all of the ingredients into the blender. Blend until smooth.

Strawberry Coconut-Smoothie

With just 5 ingredients, this dairy-free smoothie is creamy and sweet. The vanilla makes this blend taste like ice cream. I love to add a little bit of unsweetened shredded coconut after blending for added flavor.

Serves: 1
Prep. Time: 3 minutes
Blend Time: 2 minutes

Nutritional Facts
Serving Size: 219 g

Calories: 438
Total Fat: 31 g
Saturated Fat: 25.7 g   **Trans. Fat:** 0 g
Cholesterol: 0 mg
Sodium: 76 mg
Potassium: 475 mg
Total Carbohydrates: 13.8 g
Dietary Fiber: 5.7 g   **Sugar:** 7.6 g
Protein: 28.4 g
Vitamin A: 0%   **Vitamin C:** 64%
Calcium: 5%   **Iron:** 25%

Ingredients:
- 5 strawberries, frozen
- 1 cup unsweetened coconut milk
- 1 tablespoon ground flax seed

- 1 pack gelatin or 1 scoop isolate protein
- 1 teaspoon vanilla extract

Directions :
1. Put all of the ingredients into the blender. Blend until smooth.

Coconut Chocolate Tofu Power Smoothie

This high fat, high protein smoothie tastes like a chocolate milkshake. The tofu makes this smoothie silky smooth, almost like pudding. This drink is a yummy way to start the day!

Serves: 1
Prep. Time: 3 minutes
Blend Time: 2 minutes

Nutritional Facts

Serving Size: 395 g

Calories: 401
Total Fat: 25.4 g
Saturated Fat: 18.7 g   **Trans. Fat:** 0 g
Cholesterol: 0 mg
Sodium: 88 mg
Potassium: 488 mg
Total Carbohydrates: 13.6 g
Dietary Fiber: 4.7 g   **Sugar:** 7.6 g
Protein: 37.2 g
Vitamin A: 0%   **Vitamin C:** 4%
Calcium: 29%   **Iron:** 25%

Ingredients:

- 80 ml unsweetened coconut milk
- 1/2 cup tofu, silken

- 1 tablespoon unsweetened cocoa powder
- 150 ml water
- 1 packet Stevia
- 1 pack gelatin or 1 scoop isolate protein

Directions :
1. Put all of the ingredients into the blender. Blend until smooth.

Conclusion

Thank you again for downloading this book. I hope this book was able to help you to start and stay on a Ketogenic Diet. The next step is to just get going!

Finally, if you enjoyed this book I'd like to ask you to leave a review for this book on Amazon, it would be greatly appreciated!

I am constantly looking for way to improve my content to give readers the best value so If you didn't like the book I would like to also hear from you:

Twitter: @JeremyStoneEat

Thank you and good luck!

CPSIA information can be obtained
at www.ICGtesting.com
Printed in the USA
LVOW01s1035270916
506382LV00015B/356/P